New York Management Law

New York Management Law:

*The Practical Guide to Employment Law
for Business Owners and Managers*

Scott Horton

MODERN
LEGAL
MEDIA

Modern Legal Media, LLC
P.O. Box 981
Orchard Park, NY 14127
www.modernlegalmedia.com

Nothing in this book may be considered as the rendering of legal advice for specific cases. All readers are responsible for obtaining advice from their own legal counsel. This book is intended for educational and information purposes only. The author and publisher are not liable if the reader relied on the material and was financially damaged in some way.

For information about special discounts available for bulk purchases, sales promotions, and educational needs, contact the publisher.

Printed in the United States of America

First Edition

ISBN: 978-1-7322447-8-8 (paperback)
ISBN: 978-1-7322447-3-3 (e-book)

10 9 8 7 6 5 4 3 2 1

For Jen, Andrew, and Danielle
with thanks and love.
Your inspiration means the world.

Table of Contents

INTRODUCTION

As reflected by the subtitle, this book was not written for employment lawyers. (Though many of them would likely find it helpful.) It intentionally avoids legal citations. It is not comprehensive—for two reasons.

One, if I tried to address every aspect of labor and employment law affecting New York employers, the book would be too unwieldy to read. And I want people to read it. Don't just shove it on the bookshelf and think of it as a reference guide. The real benefit is in reading it like you would other self-improvement style non-fiction books. Read it to obtain a good background knowledge of relevant concepts and then refer back when employee issues arise. (Of course, you're welcome to skip portions of the book that talk about issues that don't apply to you. But, I suggest that you at least read enough to be confident they don't apply before moving along!)

Two, the underlying laws change frequently. If I'm lucky, none of the material mentioned in this book will be out-of-date by the time it is published. But some will be sooner or later. My goal is that occasional changes in the law don't render this book obsolete as a foundational reference for businesses operating in New York State.

If you want or need legal citations, there are other resources available. But keep in mind that all of them are prone to being inaccurate—either because of original editorial mistakes or due to unaccounted-for legal developments. If you get to the point where the details matter that much, you should probably be speaking to an experienced labor and employment attorney anyway. (Note: All direct quotations are from public documents, primarily statutes and regulations. If you need a citation, just Google the phrases of interest. If that doesn't work for some reason, contact me and I'll help you out.)

The book highlights New York employment laws and was written primarily for businesses with employees in New York. However, many of the lessons here apply in other states as well— especially since much of the content addresses federal U.S. labor and employment laws. Thus, the book should still be quite useful for companies with some of their workforce outside of New York.

Although written by a New York State-licensed attorney, nothing in this book qualifies as legal advice specific to any organization. Because individual situations differ in many facets, it is impossible to render one-size-fits-all professional advice; instead, this book only provides general information designed to be useful to its readers, who are trusted and encouraged to consult with appropriate legal counsel when warranted.

To eliminate any doubt: THIS BOOK CREATES NO ATTORNEY-CLIENT RELATIONSHIP BETWEEN THE AUTHOR OR PUBLISHER AND ITS READERS.

In the first chapter I begin with some overall concepts related to employment law and the workplace. I walk through aspects of preparing for and then hiring employees. Then I offer some critical guidance for all employers. If you're really crunched for time, try to at least get through this first chapter as a primer. Ideally, it will peak your interest in some of the issues that follow.

Chapter 2 digs into the critical subject of wage and hour laws. Just as compensation is fundamental to any employment relationship, the laws related to paying employees carry primary importance. Employers who fail to follow these requirements often run into problems with state agencies or individual employees. Increasingly, attorneys for employees also like to litigate, preferably in class actions, over these issues, because they can recover substantial attorneys' fees even for relatively technical violations.

I spend Chapter 3 talking about a single New York State law—the Paid Family Leave Benefits Law (plus some related issues under the federal Family and Medical Leave Act). I give this area of law so much attention because the New York law just took effect at the beginning of 2018 and affects virtually all private-sector employers in the state.

Together Chapters 4 and 5 address many aspects of discrimination law. Chapter 4 introduces various basic employment discrimination principles and describes some New York-specific rights and restrictions. Chapter 5 focuses more specifically on workplace harassment, including sexual harassment. Chapter 5 also includes information about anti-harassment training and responding to discrimination complaints.

Chapter 6 introduces concepts related to labor relations. This includes discussion about dealing with unions. But it also describes additional implications of the federal National Labor

Relations Act, which does more than just give employees the right to organize.

Finally, Chapter 7 concludes the primary content of the book on the subject of ending the employment relationship. There I seek to empower employers to move on from workers when necessary, notwithstanding the myriad landmines (including the many identified earlier in the book). And I offer guidance on how, perhaps, to accomplish the unpleasant task.

The end of the book also includes appendices that provide additional useful information in a quick-reference format. Familiarizing yourself with that material should alone launch you ahead of many of your counterparts toward understanding the laws of the workplace.

CHAPTER 1-GETTING STARTED

Most reading this are probably in organizations that already have employees. Don't skip this first chapter, even though it uses examples of initial workforce design and hiring a business's first employees. Virtually all the contents of this chapter apply to hiring your *next* employee as well.

Workforce Design Meets Employment Law

Let's say you are an entrepreneur. You have a product or service worth buying, and maybe you're already selling it. But now you need to build a team to help your business really take off. What legal issues should you keep in mind when you consider your workforce design?

Yes, I'm an employment lawyer. No, I'm not suggesting that employment laws should be the primary factor in how you organize the people in your company. But once you have employees, complying with employment laws enters the equation.

Why Should You Design Your Workforce?

What are we talking about anyway? Maybe one day you could literally design the people in your workforce if you wanted to. They could all be robots. You could order the precise models and styles you want.

I don't know if employment laws will eventually apply to robots. I kind of doubt it, and hope not, I think. (Then again, that would help keep people like me relevant despite a robot revolution . . . but I digress.)

If you want your business to work and grow, you want the right people involved. And even if you have the right people, they need some direction and scope of responsibilities. We're not going to get into the weeds of titles and job descriptions here. Those aren't all that critical to the first issues I have in mind. Still, if your employees don't have direction, you'll have chaos.

Okay, perhaps chaos works for you. But it doesn't work for most businesses. And it doesn't avoid the obligation to comply with employment laws. (If you're interested in the type of chaos that includes disregard of employment laws, then why are you reading this book? Anyway, good luck. But there's a list of government websites in Appendix A that you should be aware of!)

So, I assume those who are still reading value some structure. Each person reports to someone else. People will have some physical space to work in (though it may not be on company premises). There must be some rules about what employees can and can't do. (You're not going to give everyone access to the bank accounts, right?) You'll need to address compensation, including guarantees, expectations, and logistics.

That's probably just the tip of the iceberg. But it's enough to get us started here.

How Do You Design Your Workforce?

WARNING: This is not intended to be a blueprint. Any good workforce design needs to focus specifically on your business. We can't tackle that in the abstract. But I think some examples will be helpful.

How much can you spend?

Suppose you've spent six months working by yourself to launch your business. Good news: It's working! You decide that you can afford to spend $150,000 on a staff over the next year. You'll re-evaluate after that (or, more likely, earlier, but let's keep this relatively simple!).

Well, now you must decide how to spend that $150,000.

First, remember that not all the $150,000 will end up in the hands of your employees. Most likely you at least must get a workers' compensation insurance policy. In New York, you'll also need disability benefits insurance. And there's unemployment insurance. Plus, of course, taxes: FICA, FUTA, income tax withholdings. Oh, and did you want to offer your employees health insurance, life insurance, etc.?

You could try to avoid some of those items by hiring independent contractors, but then you're taking the risk of misclassification. (More on that later!) Many workers treated as independent contractors are indeed employees under relevant laws. That means you may expose yourself to additional penalties for not providing/deducting all the items in the previous paragraph. That's not to say you should never use independent contractors—I don't assume you'll have a full-time plumber/electrician on staff—but for now, we'll stick with direct employees.

How many employees do you want?

Just to keep the numbers round, we'll say you'll end up with $100,000 in real after-tax cash (which you'll pay by check or direct deposit, but you get the point) to offer workers over the next year. How do you want to spread that around? Give it all to one person? Rotate through 10 low-paid part-timers?

Believe it or not, employment laws may play a significant role in this crucial workforce design decision. Minimum wage and overtime are obvious factors. There's also the fact (as you'll learn) that some legal obligations depend on the number of employees you have.

To move things along, let's go with an initial workforce of three employees. We'll have one full-time employee and two part-timers.

There are still many workforce design questions to answer, such as:

- What do full- and part-time mean?
- How will they be paid?
- When will they work?
- Where will they work?
- What will they do?
- What will they use?

Workforce Design Meets Employment Law

Let's take each of the specific questions above and look at how employment law may influence your decisions.

1. What do full- and part-time mean?

The law doesn't directly dictate this. Typically, full-time is 40+ hours. But sometimes it's 35 or 37.5 hours, depending on the length of an unpaid lunch period. And those are only some possibilities.

However, there are laws that apply differently depending on whether an employee is full- or part-time, as defined by the law in question.

The federal and New York workforce reduction laws (the "WARN" Acts, see Chapter 7), for example, use 20 hours per week as the cutoff for part-time workers. So does the New York Paid Family Leave Benefits Law.

Under the Affordable Care Act (ACA), or "Obamacare," a worker is full-time if they work 30+ hours per week.

Just looking at those examples, the WARN Acts and the ACA don't apply to businesses with only three employees (referencing our scenario above). But the New York Paid Family Leave Benefits Law does, even if only one of the three employees works in New York! If you're trying to structure your New York workforce so employees won't be eligible to take paid family leave, then you would need to limit considerably their days and hours worked. (Don't worry, there's a whole chapter on New York Paid Family Leave coming up later!)

2. How will they be paid?

What if you don't want to pay overtime? Then you have two options. One is not to let anyone work over 40 hours in a week. The other is to qualify your employees for an exemption to overtime requirements.

Not everyone can be appropriately classified as exempt. It depends, in part, on what someone does in their job. But for most exemptions, the employee also must be paid on a salary basis. The federal salary threshold is in flux (as we'll discuss). So, let's just start with New York law.

In 2018, an employer with less than 10 employees must pay a New York City-based employee at least $900/week to satisfy the most common exemptions. If you're going to pay that much so you don't have to pay overtime when they work 50 hours in a week, are you willing to let them have weeks where they only work 30 hours? Or do you need 50 hours of work each week to justify the salary?

And look—if you have around $100,000 to pay three people, you can't afford to have all three of them be exempt if they work in New York City. But if they work somewhere with a lower exemption salary requirement, then maybe you could, if their job duties qualify.

3. When will they work?

This ties back to the last problem. You can't just say work whenever. Sure, you might have employees that don't work enough. But the more significant problem, especially if you hired hard workers, is that they'll work too much. Then you'll be stuck paying overtime you can't afford.

New York law also requires meal periods. This may prohibit you from having an employee work when you otherwise would like them to. (We'll discuss further.)

In some industries, such as trucking, there are also specific requirements for how long an employee can work (which are beyond the scope of this book).

4. Where will they work?

Do you have space for them in your office or facility? Can they work at home? Will they need to travel? Who will pay for that?

Remember, especially for non-exempt employees, you must track time worked. The traditional time clock may be a helpful tool. Time can be harder to track for employees who are offsite. But there are plenty of technology-based solutions to monitor time. These could range from an email where the employee self-reports time worked on a periodic basis to software that records when the employee logs into and out of their computer. Which methods will you use?

There are also overtime rules that apply in determining whether you must pay employees for time spent traveling related to work. (Keep reading.)

And don't forget access issues. If employees will be working in your facility when you aren't there, how will they get in? Do they need to lock up when they leave?

5. What will they do?

Sure, job descriptions are helpful. You can write those up front, before you hire. Or you can bring on the right people and figure out how they fit best. Whether written down or not, the scope of an employee's job matters for employment law purposes.

First, there are the overtime exemptions. They almost always depend, in part, on what the employee does. It's not enough to call someone the Vice President of Sales and assume they're exempt. If this employee only enters customer data into a spreadsheet, they're probably not going to qualify for an exemption.

Next, if you have enough employees to be subject to disability discrimination laws (15 or more under the Americans with Disabilities Act (ADA); only four under the New York State and City Human Rights Laws), you may end up having to determine the "essential functions" of a person's job. The ADA and the New

York Human Rights Laws protect employees who can perform the essential functions of their job with or without reasonable accommodations.

What if an employee's disability prevents him from driving? Suppose you want your employees to be able to drive to visit customers, run errands, etc. If that's only incidental to their primary responsibilities, then you may not be able just to get rid of the employee who can't drive due to disability.

There can even be union-related considerations in workforce design. Maybe you don't want a union. (We address that in Chapter 6.) But what if your new employees do. Even at just three employees, they could try to unionize. However, if you're an employer subject to the National Labor Relations Act (NLRA), a bona fide "supervisor" isn't eligible to be in a union. The NLRA's other protections don't apply to supervisors either. But, again, just calling someone a supervisor doesn't make it so in the eyes of the law. It will depend on what they actually do in the course of their job.

6. What will they use?

Maybe you have a residential lawn care company. If so, you may only entrust employees to use a push mower and hedge clippers. No big deal. You just have to make sure they're safe in compliance with the Occupational Safety and Health Act (OSHA).

But, if you're in a technology field, medicine, or consulting, the stakes may be higher. Are you providing a computer? Access to proprietary databases? In these situations, you'll want to consider how to protect your assets, and those of your clients, even from your own employees. Confidentiality agreements and even non-competes may be appropriate.

And if you run a factory, for example, your safety requirements under OSHA will be more involved.

No Shortcuts to Workforce Design

Most business owners and managers won't sit down and think through every possible legal issue related to bringing on a workforce. There are plenty of limitations on time and resources when confronting workforce design. But, employment law compliance shouldn't be an afterthought.

Larger, more established companies may have more resources and experience with having employees. But that's not a complete advantage. That means they also have inertia going against them. In many ways, it's easier to design your workforce from scratch than reorganize an existing staff.

Regardless, it's unlikely that any business will get workforce design exactly right the first time, or any time. You will learn from what works and what doesn't and adjust accordingly. You will also gain more experience with how the various employment laws may affect you. Learn from that too.

Hiring Your First (or Next) Employee in New York

Now that your business is ready for employees (or more employees), it's time to hire. Although I know many readers are in organizations that already have employees in New York, let's just assume for a moment that yours doesn't. This approach will both lay a roadmap for first-time employers and enable existing employers to perform a checkup on their hiring practices.

There are three general scenarios for a business hiring its first employee in New York State:

1. A New York-based company is hiring its first employee overall.
2. A company that already has one or more employees in another state is hiring its first employee in New York.
3. A foreign company is hiring its first U.S. employee, who will work in New York.

I have represented employers in each scenario. Some issues are the same across the board. Others differ.

Here's an overview of the considerations in each situation. As always, don't rely entirely on this book to guide your hiring process. You should seek legal and other assistance to ensure compliance.

First Employee Overall

Some businesses start out with employees. Others are run entirely by the owner(s) until they decide to hire someone to help run the business. Either way, once the first non-owner comes on board, the business (or its owner(s) personally) becomes an employer. Having employees can be great for many reasons, but being an employer imposes many new requirements.

As an employer, you now (in most cases) must arrange several kinds of mandatory insurance: workers' compensation, unemployment, and (in New York) short-term disability. Failure to immediately obtain these insurance coverages can result in significant liability.

Other forms of employee insurance are technically optional. These include health insurance and life insurance. Many small employers do not provide these benefits, but many others do. Unless you need to offer these to attract the employees you're trying to hire, these benefits should not be your first concern. Get the statutorily required insurances first. And make sure you comply with the other notice and recordkeeping requirements that now apply to your business.

Once you are an employer, you also become subject to various notice posting requirements. For example, all employers must post information in the workplace about minimum wage and overtime requirements. Some posting requirements depend on the number of employees you have, either in the state, in the United States, or overall. All required notices are probably available online through the various enforcement agencies, but many employers obtain posters from private vendors. In either case, you must ensure that you have all necessary (and current) postings up based on your size and location(s).

First Employee in New York

Even if your company already has employees in other U.S. states, New York has its own specific requirements. If you have an employee based in New York, you probably must satisfy most of these to avoid potential liability.

These include obtaining the disability insurance coverage mentioned above. Whereas most states require workers' compensation insurance, New York is one of only five states that require this coverage. It partially compensates employees unable to work based on a non-work illness/injury. (California, Hawaii, New Jersey, and Rhode Island have similar requirements.)

New York also has specific wage notice requirements. Each employee in New York must receive written notice of certain information about their employer and their compensation. The employee must sign and return a copy, and the employer must retain the copy in its files. Moreover, if the employee's primary language is one other than English, the notice may have to be provided in that language. Finally, changes in compensation or company information may require employers to give employees new notices. (More details in the next chapter!)

Upon hiring an employee in New York, you must also notify the State that you have done so. You can find more information about that at https://www.tax.ny.gov/bus/wt/newhire.htm.

Some requirements depend on where within New York the employee works. Most of these relate to employees in New York City. For example, New York City has a paid sick leave law that requires employers to notify employees of their sick leave rights.

First Employee in the United States

Some requirements will apply to all employees in the United States, whether in New York or another state.

Employers must obtain and retain a completed I-9 form for each employee hired after November 6, 1986. This form confirms the individual's eligibility to work in the United States. In addition to providing information on the form, employees must show documentation establishing their right to work. This may include drivers' licenses, passports, social security cards, visas, etc. Allowing an employee to work without completing the form in the first three days of employment creates significant legal exposure under U.S. immigration laws.

Employees should also complete a W-4 form to enable the employer to make appropriate tax deductions from their compensation. Many states also impose income taxes and may have their own employee withholding form. (In New York, it's the IT-2104 form.) Failure to properly deduct income taxes can create problems for both the employer and the employee.

Finally, the Fair Labor Standards Act establishes both a minimum wage (currently $7.25 per hour) and overtime requirements (generally time-and-a-half pay for hours worked beyond 40 in a week). Many states have similar laws that may impose higher wage requirements (as is the case in New York). Some employees, however, are exempt from minimum wage or overtime pay requirements. Be sure you know how these (complicated) laws affect your employee(s) before bringing them on board. (We'll spend much of the next chapter on this!)

Don't Stop Here

If you are hiring your first (or next) employee in New York (or anywhere else), make sure you thoroughly consider all the legal and financial implications. They are not all mentioned here, but hopefully, this is a good place to start. Most companies should speak to both an accountant and an employment lawyer before adding their first employees. Those hiring *more* employees should beware thresholds that implicate additional legal parameters. (Many are discussed in this book.) Being proactive here can save your business considerably in the long run.

Don't Ask These Questions During Job Interviews

Now that you're hiring, either for the first or umpteenth time, you get to wade through an array of legal minefields.

For example, various federal and state laws affect what questions employers may ask during job interviews. These laws are designed to prevent employment discrimination.

Here are some questions you usually may **NOT** ask.

Prohibited Questions

Age

- How old are you?
- What is your date of birth?
- When did you graduate high school?

Disability

- Do you have a disability?
- Have you ever had a drug or alcohol problem?
- Have you ever been treated for any diseases?

Family

- Are you married?
- Do you have kids? Plan to?
- Are you pregnant?
- Do any of your family members have any serious medical conditions?

Race/National Origin

- What race do you identify with?
- What country are you from?
- Where were your parents born?
- What is your native language?

Religion

- What church do you attend?
- Do you pray?
- Do you observe any religious holidays?

Permissible Questions

By contrast, here are some questions you generally may ask, if relevant, during job interviews:

- Are you 18 years or older?
- Have you ever been convicted of a crime?
- Does your spouse work here?
- Are you eligible to work in the United States?
- What schools did you attend?
- What degrees or certifications have your earned?
- Do you speak [language used in the job]?
- How long have you lived in this area?

Subtle Differences Matter

Sometimes the precise wording of the question makes all the difference. For example, it's okay to verify that someone is old enough to work, but not acceptable to ask how old they are. However, if it's clear that the person is still young enough that availability to work may depend on their precise age, then asking their age directly may be okay. This would usually only apply to the youngest workers (i.e., under 18), where child labor laws apply.

Similarly, most questions about a candidate's family situation are risky. They could touch on various protected characteristics, including sex, disability, genetic information, religion, etc. However, employers can ask during job interviews whether the candidate has any family members that already work at the company. Some employers even have anti-nepotism policies or other restrictions on multiple family members working together. Such rules usually do not violate any laws if applied consistently.

Job Interviews Should Focus on Candidates' Ability to Do the Job

The best way to avoid asking a problematic question during a job interview is to focus solely on the ability to perform the job.

Obviously, there are many different jobs, so there is no single right way to interview candidates. But all interviewers should try to ignore age, sex, race, national origin, religion, etc. That doesn't mean they can completely overcome stereotypes, subtle biases, etc. But at least they must keep that off the table during job interviews.

Check for Discriminatory Impact

Especially where a relatively large number of employees are hired into similar positions, hiring decisions can be reviewed statistically to see if there are any discriminatory trends. If a disproportionate number of applicants of a certain race, sex, or age are being hired into the company or job groups, then further analysis may be warranted. In some cases, this may show that particular interviewers are asking the wrong questions.

Smaller employers or those with less turnover can't test for statistical significance as reliably. But since there are relatively few positions, it is easier to look at each hiring decision individually to check whether any potential discrimination has filtered into the job interviews.

Most often, even if an interviewer has crossed the line by asking an inappropriate question, no significant harm will occur. Counsel the interviewer on the error and instruct them how to avoid making the same mistake in the future.

If, however, an applicant or employee does make a discrimination complaint, then make sure you respond appropriately. (We discuss responding to discrimination complaints in Chapter 5.)

Employee Classification Mistakes

Finding the right workers is one thing. Once they agree to join the workforce, the company must process them for administrative purposes. This isn't always as straightforward as it may seem.

Let's face it—most organizations are in business to do something other than worry about how they classify their employees. They have products or services to offer, and they want to do so efficiently and effectively. Unfortunately, because it's not their area of expertise, many businesses make employee classification errors despite their good intentions. But, here's an opportunity to correct those mistakes!

These are five of the most common employee classification mistakes I see from good companies trying to do the right thing.

1. Contract Designation vs. Legal Reality

Perhaps the first lesson in employment law should be "just because it's on paper, doesn't make it so!" One area this applies is the threshold question of whether a worker is an employee or an independent contractor. Often, businesses and workers prefer the "independent contractor" designation for assorted reasons. So, they execute a contract that says that the person is not an employee of the company. Unfortunately, it's not that easy.

It turns out that a lot of government entities care about the "independent contractor" vs. "employee" classification. This includes the IRS and state taxing authorities, state unemployment and workers' compensation authorities, departments of labor and other agencies enforcing labor and employment laws, and the courts. And, usually, the government has (financial) incentive (e.g., taxes) to find a worker to be an "employee."

Frankly, having a piece of paper that says a person is not an employee tends to be one of the least relevant factors in this determination. It's nice to have, and you do want to have a written contract if you're trying to prove an independent contractor relationship. But the government looks at many aspects of the relationship to evaluate whether the worker qualifies as an employee under whatever law is in question (e.g., minimum wage, employment tax withholding, etc.).

Some factors that matter more than words on the page include:

- Who provides the tools and equipment the worker uses?

- Does the worker operate a business and have other customers?

- Does the worker control the timing and means of getting the work done?

- Is the worker directly involved in the company's core functions or just enabling the company to operate its business?

Cautious companies will consider these and other questions carefully before entering into an agreement with a potential independent contractor. The agreement should confirm the factors that will support the classification. But, again, the contract itself won't be the deciding factor.

2. "Salary" vs. "Hourly"

Sure, it's fine to classify some employees as "salary" and others as "hourly." But these categories only go so far. One of the most common employee classification mistakes is equating salaried with "exempt" and hourly with "non-exempt" for overtime purposes.

Paying an employee a salary does not automatically exempt them from receiving overtime under the Fair Labor Standards Act (FLSA) and state laws. And, it goes the other way too. Some hourly employees can still be exempt from overtime (though this is less common).

The most prevalent overtime exemptions are the so-called "white collar" exemptions. These include administrative, executive, professional, computer employee, and outside sales exemptions. Some exemptions require that employees be paid on a salary basis. But that is never the *only* requirement! The nature of the employee's work must also satisfy certain tests. Moreover, the FLSA has no salary requirement for the outside sales exemption and certain professional categories (doctor, lawyer, and teacher). And qualifying computer employees can be exempt even if they receive an hourly wage. (Chapter 2 discusses these exemptions under the FLSA and New York law in much more detail.)

3. "Full-time" vs. "Part-time"

Again, this is a useful designation. But it's not a one-size-fits-all classification. Even within the same workplace, two "full-time" employees may work different schedules and total numbers of hours in a week. The same may be true for two "part-time" employees.

Like with "salary" vs. "hourly," "full-time" vs. "part-time" doesn't necessarily signify whether an employee is eligible to receive overtime pay.

When labor and employment laws use these or similar terms, they mean different things depending on the law. As mentioned before, the ACA defines full-time to mean the employee works an average of 30 hours per week, and other prevalent New York and federal laws draw the line at 20 hours per week. And these are just some examples.

It's important for employers to understand the context in which a particular employee is part-time or full-time. Day-to-day, the distinction probably depends not on external laws, but on how the company itself defines the categories, such as for employee benefits eligibility like vacation and holiday pay. But understand that failing to draw the correct line for specific legal analyses is another of the most problematic employee classification mistakes.

4. Job Description vs. Actual Duties

For employment law purposes, there are many reasons why it may matter what an employee's job entails. Most of the time that inquiry should not end with reviewing a written job description. Like the written designation of a worker as an independent contractor instead of an employee, words on a page describing what the employee's position entails are seldom determinative. Instead, you must know what this specific person actually does for the organization.

For starters, this is critical in classifying employees as exempt vs. non-exempt. It also comes into play in determining essential functions of an employee's position for disability accommodation purposes.

Yes, it's nice when the written job description accurately reflects the work that the employee in fact performs. And this is a good reason to review and update your job descriptions regularly. But organizations often prepare a job description when they create a position and then use it for years without reevaluating. The employees in the role probably have changed, as have the exact tasks of the job.

5. Union vs. Non-Union

The last of these employee classification mistakes is only relevant if a union represents (or perhaps is seeking to represent) some of your employees. That's a diminishing percentage of U.S. workplaces, but still a significant number of them.

Obviously, it is essential to know which employees are in the union bargaining unit and which are not. Especially in right-to-work states—New York is not one—that isn't necessarily the same as which employees are technically members of the union. But, regardless, if they are in the bargaining unit, then the employer must deal with the union directly rather than the employee regarding certain matters.

Like some other employee classification mistakes above, "union" vs. "nonunion" does not legally equate to whether an employee is exempt or non-exempt from overtime. Or whether they are protected by federal or state leave laws or other benefits matters.

Typically, having unionized employees just adds another layer to an already complex web of labor and employment law compliance issues. It is often critical to break out the pieces of the web to analyze and address them properly.

Avoiding Employee Classification Mistakes

Yes, the best way for most organizations to avoid costly employee classification mistakes is to consult with an experienced labor and employment lawyer. But, admittedly, it's hard to know when you are wandering into a trap for the unwary such that legal advice is necessary. This book should help you better understand where the biggest trouble spots lie. The next section illustrates more of these.

Bad Business Ideas for Good Employers

You're in charge of managing a workforce. Maybe you own the company. Or you could be in human resources. Or another aspect of management. I assume you want to be considered one of the good employers, right?

In that case, here are five things you should never do!

1. Date Subordinates

Okay, you know what I'm talking about. But let's start with what I'm not talking about. Especially if you own or help operate a small business, it's reasonable that your spouse or longtime partner may also become involved. I'm not strictly advocating "no nepotism" policies. But don't cross dangerous lines needlessly!

No matter how well you and your direct reports get along, it must stay professional, or at most friendly. Dating, where it could become romantic, isn't worth the risk. Sure, it might work out great. But there are many ways it could go south.

First, advances may be rebuffed. If that happens, then the relationship between the two of you may be permanently tainted.

Second, even if a relationship develops, what are the motives? Is your employee only dating you to keep the job, to get ahead, to set you up? This just isn't the right way to look for love!

Third, even if the relationship is real and works out, other employees may not like it. They might see it as creating a bias in favor of the employee you're dating. And, let's face it, you probably would—even should—be biased in that situation. What happens if the employee's performance drops below an acceptable level and you must fire your significant other?

Fourth, sexual harassment claims. By your desired paramour. From other employees. And these could come months or years down the road. You don't need me to tell you that these claims are a big strike against otherwise good employers!

If you nonetheless find yourself dating an employee that reports to you, figure out a way to minimize the risk. Yes, there are even so-called "love contracts" where both parties make representations in writing to help the employer avoid liability. Hopefully, you don't have to go that far. Reassigning the employee may solve, or at least help, the problem. But don't just assume you can date an employee and have everything go smoothly. It probably won't.

2. Keep Problem Employees

Any business with multiple employees over time will eventually end up with a bad one. This doesn't necessarily mean someone with bad motives, though it can. More often, it's just an employee who isn't the right fit for the job for whatever reasons.

Some good employers think they can right the ship no matter what. "I hired this guy. I can fix him." But that philosophy doesn't always work. Okay, it usually doesn't.

Even if you could retrain a chronically underperforming employee, it probably isn't worth the effort. You could find someone else better out there right now.

And if someone lies to you once or twice, can you afford to give them another chance?

You don't need to have a one-strike policy in all respects. But you must be realistic. If someone isn't the right fit now, they probably won't be in six months either.

Here's another secret. The longer you employ someone, the more it costs to get rid of them. There are many inputs in this calculation. They may include training costs, severance pay, the risk of litigation, etc. Do the analysis earlier rather than later, compare the cost of trying someone else, and make the difficult decision. You'll be glad you did.

3. Hire People Like You

We are all predisposed to like people who resemble us. We're automatically more comfortable and familiar with them. We know how they think, how they behave, and what motivates them. Or, at least we assume we do.

However, there are two significant problems with hiring based on similarities.

The first is a legal concern. Discrimination. If you only hire/promote people similar to you in race, age, gender, etc., then you may be systematically disadvantaging particular classes of candidates. This can mean litigation, legal fees, and settlements or damages awards. Not good, obviously.

The second is a business concern. Do you really need more people like you? You already do "you" better than anyone else. What you need is a mix of "not-yous" to complement your strengths and weaknesses.

This doesn't mean you can or should only hire people who are nothing like you. To be sure, only hiring employees of a different race or sex may also constitute discrimination. But good employers embrace diversity of experience, personality, characteristics, etc., not just because it's the right thing to do, but because it works for their business too!

4. Ignore Complaints

No one is perfect. Your business will make mistakes, or at least the people working for you will. It's better to foster a culture where people are open about their mistakes so that they can be corrected. Otherwise, they build on themselves, making matters worse.

So, how do you foster this positive culture? First, don't overreact. Try not to scream or disparage someone when you find out they did something wrong. If this is merely a performance matter, then try to correct it and move on. Obviously, consistently poor performance is another issue, addressed above (and in Chapter 7).

Now, let's say you discover a mistake because another person files a complaint. And let's say this complaint alleges harassment, discrimination, or other mistreatment. Then the organization must investigate, but, again, don't overreact.

Just because someone complains about a co-worker, it doesn't always mean they want to sue the company. Often the investigation will reveal a misunderstanding that can be remedied. Other times, you may discover that someone has crossed the line. But even then it doesn't necessarily mean they meant to. Where possible, correct the mistake and make sure it doesn't happen again.

Especially in the harassment context (sexual, racial, age-based, etc.), the potential liability often arises once an employer knows of misconduct and fails to act. But acting doesn't always have to mean firing anyone, or even transferring employees. Sometimes the investigation may be sufficient.

If you don't take a complaint seriously or don't try to get to the bottom of things, then you create a big target if the unwelcome behavior persists. Yes, this often increases the employer's legal responsibility for this conduct. More important, it increases the likelihood that the complaining employee will go outside the company to seek redress.

Be prepared for these situations in advance.

5. Forego Overtime Pay

Overtime is a major compensation issue that many employers, including good ones, get wrong. Yes, it's nice to have employees willing to work as much as you need them to. But if you don't pay them as required, it can cost you tremendously.

Lawyers representing employees are eager to sue employers for failure to pay overtime. Not only can they recover handsomely for their clients. They also receive their fees from the employer if they win. Don't be a target for these lawyers. Do it right!

The basic rule is that employees who work over 40 hours in a week must be paid overtime at time-and-a-half. Some employees can be exempt, meaning they need not receive overtime pay. And, in some cases, different hour thresholds and payment requirements apply.

Here are some of the common mistakes:

- Not accurately recording all hours worked.

- Not paying overtime when earned.

- Providing "comp time" instead of overtime pay, which isn't allowed for non-governmental employers.

- Improperly classifying an employee as exempt.

- Miscalculating the overtime rate.

Remember, employees can't simply agree not to receive pay for overtime. The law requires it, so any such agreement probably won't hold up. If there is a claim in court or with the U.S. or New York Department of Labor, then it's the employer's burden to show compliance with the laws.

About those laws. . . .

CHAPTER 2—WAGE AND HOUR LAWS

When employment lawyers talk about "wage and hour" laws, they're lumping together a bunch of rules about when and how employees work and get paid. These includes minimum wage and overtime laws. It also includes laws about pay frequency, meal periods, and deductions from wages.

This book would get really boring if I tried to explain every aspect of wage and hour laws that apply to New York employers. So, I won't. But we will cover many of the issues most likely to affect your workplace on a regular basis.

Wage Notice Requirements

The New York Wage Theft Prevention Act took effect in 2011 to much fanfare. Among other things, the law required employers to give specific New York wage notices to their employees. The law originally required the notices to be given in three situations:

1. Within 10 days of hire.

2. When the information in the notice changes.

3. Annually, between January 1st and February 1st.

To the relief of businesses throughout the state, the law was amended in 2015 to no longer require the burdensome annual notice. However, employers still must give compliant wage notices to all new employees. New notices are also still required for most changes in the mandatory information.

Businesses do not have to give these notices to true independent contractors. However, as discussed, be sure that you are not treating someone as an independent contractor if they should be considered an employee.

Required Elements of New York Wage Notices

To comply with the law, the wage notices must include:

- Rate or rates of pay, including overtime rate of pay (if it applies);

- How the employee is paid: by the hour, shift, day, week, commission, etc.;

- Regular payday;

- Official name of the employer and any other names used for business (e.g., DBAs);

- Address and phone number of the employer's main office or principal location; and

- Allowances taken as part of the minimum wage (tips, meal, and lodging deductions).

(Additional notice requirements may apply to employees in the "hospitality industry"—i.e., restaurants and hotels.)

The New York State Department of Labor (NYS DOL) has created wage notices covering various employment situations. For example, there is a notice for employees paid hourly and a different notice for salaried, exempt employees. The sample notices are available on the NYS DOL's website (see Appendix A).

Employers must provide the notice in the employee's primary language if the NYS DOL has created a template notice in that language. They currently offer translations in at least these languages: Chinese, Haitian Creole, Italian, Korean, Polish, Russian, and Spanish.

In addition to providing the written notice, the employer must get a copy signed by the employee and retain it for at least six years.

When Is a New Notice Required During Employment?

If any of the required information in the New York wage notice changes, then the employer must provide a new notice and have the employee sign it.

However, the NYS DOL takes the position that except for employers in the hospitality industry, notice is not required where there is an increase in a wage/salary rate and the new rate is shown on the next wage statement (i.e., check stub). For any wage rate reduction, an employee must be notified in writing before the employer reduces the rate. Employers in the hospitality industry must give a new notice every time a wage rate changes.

It is not necessarily a bad practice to obtain a newly signed wage notice even for wage/salary increases to ensure that the employee's file always contains a current acknowledgment of the appropriate compensation rate. But this is not required (outside of the hospitality industry) and might not always be worth the administrative hassle.

What Is the Penalty for Not Providing Wage Notices?

The NYS DOL can assess damages of $50.00 per day per worker if a proper New York wage notice is not given.

Employees can also sue for damages on their own. The maximum amount an individual employee can recover is $5,000.00, and attorneys' fees and costs may also be awarded.

Wage Notice Checkup

Even if a company has only one employee who has not received timely notice, the potential penalty could be very costly. Make sure your notices are up-to-date!

Pay Frequency Laws

One component of the mandatory wage notices is the identification of the employee's regular payday.

Do you know how often you must pay your employees?

When New York employers must pay employees depends on the nature of the employee's work. Let's look at each of the categories.

Manual Workers

New York's Labor Law says that employers must pay "manual workers" weekly—more specifically, not later than seven calendar days after the end of the week in which the employee earned the wages.

The law defines "manual worker" to mean "a mechanic, workingman, or laborer."

The New York Commissioner of Labor can authorize some exceptions to this requirement. However, the exceptions are only available to non-profit organizations and for-profit companies with at least 1,000 employees in the state. The Commissioner can authorize these employers to pay manual workers no less frequently than semi-monthly.

Commissioned Salespersons

Employers must have a written compensation plan for all commissioned salespersons in New York. (The New York Labor Law uses the terms "commission salesman," "commission salesperson," and "commissioned salesperson" interchangeably. I think the last one sounds best, so I use it here.)

The law defines the terms to mean "any employee whose principal activity is the selling of any goods, wares, merchandise, services, real estate, securities, insurance or any article or thing and whose earnings are based in whole or in part on commissions." But it specifically excludes employees "whose principal activity is of a supervisory, managerial, executive or administrative nature."

The New York Labor Law also establishes alternative requirements (not discussed here) for "sales representatives" who are independent contractors rather than employees.

Both the employer and the commissioned salesperson must sign the compensation agreement. The employer must retain a copy of the agreement for at least three years.

The agreement must include:

- a description of how to calculate wages, salary, drawing account, commissions, and all other money earned and payable;

- the frequency of reconciliation for any recoverable draw; and

- details about payment of compensation earned and payable upon termination of employment by either party.

It is the employer's burden to ensure that the document is in place. Otherwise, whatever terms the commissioned salesperson says exist will likely become binding.

Employers must pay each commissioned salesperson according to the agreed terms of employment. Generally, this must be at least once per month and by the last day of the month following the month in which the employee earned the compensation. However, if monthly or more frequent payment of wages, salary, drawing accounts, or commissions are substantial, then the employer may pay additional compensation less frequently than once in each month. The employer must always pay at least as soon as required under the compensation agreement.

Upon written request of a commissioned salesperson, an employer must provide a statement of earnings paid or due and unpaid. Then an employer must pay each commissioned salesperson at least once per month, usually by the last day of the month following the month in which the commissions were earned. If there are substantial recurring monthly wages, then the employer need not pay all forms of compensation monthly. Certain additional compensation can be paid less frequently than monthly, as outlined in the compensation plan.

Other Workers

The labor law requires employers to pay "clerical and other workers" not less frequently than semi-monthly. The employer must pay these employees "in accordance with the agreed terms of employment." It must also designate regular paydays in advance.

The law defines "clerical and other worker" to mean all employees not included as manual workers, commissioned salespersons, or railroad workers. Also excluded are employees who work in a qualified executive, administrative, or professional capacity who earn more than $900 per week (for whom no specific pay frequency is required).

Final Paycheck

When an employee's employment ends, the employer must pay all wages earned by the next regular payday for the pay period during which the employment ended. This includes payout of accrued vacation or PTO pay, unless the company's policy expressly provides for forfeiture upon termination of employment.

Sometimes the employer cannot determine the final compensation by that time. For example, commissions or bonuses may depend on ongoing projects. In these cases, the employer must determine when the compensation will be earned and then pay by the applicable payday.

Deductions from Wages

New York law places many restrictions on what employers may deduct or withhold from their employees' paychecks. Of course, legally mandated deductions, such as for state and federal taxes or wage garnishments, are permitted. But most other items not for the employee's own benefit are prohibited. For example, employers may not hold back money from their employees' wages to account for cash or inventory shortfalls, even if the employer can prove the employee took the money or goods.

Permissible Deductions

The New York Labor Law generally prohibits all deductions from wages, but then allows exceptions for:

1. Deductions made in accordance with any governmental law, rule, or regulations;

2. Certain voluntary deductions expressly authorized in writing by the employee (or through a collective bargaining agreement);

3. Recovery of overpayment of wages due to a mathematical or other clerical error (subject to additional requirements); and

4. Repayment of salary/wage advancements (subject to additional requirements).

Employee Authorized Deductions

Even where the employee would agree to have money taken out of their pay, the law only permits deductions for the following purposes under category 2 above:

- Insurance premiums and prepaid legal plans;

- Pension or health and welfare plans;

- Contributions to a bona fide charitable organization;

- Certain purchases made at events sponsored by bona fide charitable organizations;

- U.S. bonds;

- Labor organization dues or assessments;

- Discounted parking or passes, tokens, fare cards, vouchers, or other items for employee use of mass transit;

- Fitness center, health club, and gym membership dues;

- On-premise cafeteria, vending machine, and gift shop purchases operated by employer hospital, college, or university;

- On-premise pharmacy purchases;

- Tuition, room, board, and fees for pre-school, nursery, primary, secondary, and post-secondary educational institutions;

- Daycare, before-school, and after-school care expenses;

- Certain housing provided by non-profit hospitals or their affiliates; and

- Similar payments for the benefit of the employee.

That last item is a doozy. What's like those other items, and what's not? Hopefully, you won't have to try to answer that question!

Minimum Wage

New York businesses usually must pay employees at least the state minimum wage for all hours worked (before factoring in lawful deductions). Most companies are also subject to the federal minimum wage and overtime requirements of the Fair Labor Standards Act (FLSA). Some employees are exempt or subject to special wage requirements.

The next sections discuss the most common minimum wage/overtime requirements for New York employers.

Standard Minimum Wage

The current U.S. minimum wage is $7.25 per hour.

The chart below shows the current minimum wage and scheduled increases, by geographic location and employer size (where applicable), for most New York private employers.

Location	12/31/17	12/31/18	12/31/19	12/31/20	2021
NYC–Large Employers (of 11 or more)	$13.00	$15.00			
NYC–Small Employers (10 or less)	$12.00	$13.50	$15.00		
Long Island & Westchester	$11.00	$12.00	$13.00	$14.00	$15.00
Remainder of New York State	$10.40	$11.10	$11.80	$12.50	TBD*

* Annual increases for the rest of the state will continue until the rate reaches a $15 minimum wage.

New York Minimum Wage for Tipped Employees in the Hospitality Industry

New York has separate minimum wage rules for employees in the hospitality industry. The hospitality industry includes any restaurant or hotel. The minimum wage for most *non-tipped* employees in the hospitality industry is set as per the schedule above. However, employers in New York (and most other states) have historically been able to count a portion of certain tipped employees' gratuities toward the minimum wage requirements. This is known as a "tip credit."

In December 2017, Governor Andrew Cuomo directed New York's Commissioner of Labor to hold public hearings to evaluate the possibility of ending minimum wage tip credits in the state. Governor Cuomo's announcement reflected his belief that New York should eliminate tip credits. The Commissioner of Labor's decision regarding tip credits is expected after July 1, 2018.

Until then, at least, New York has two separate cash wage and tip credit schedules for tipped hospitality employees who qualify as "food service workers" or "service employees."

Food Service Workers

A *food service worker* is an employee who is primarily engaged in serving food or beverages to guests, patrons, or customers in the hospitality industry who regularly receives tips. This includes wait staff, bartenders, captains, and busing personnel.

This chart shows the minimum cash wage and maximum tip credit for these employees. (Minimum cash wage listed first.)

Location	12/31/17	12/31/18	12/31/19	12/31/20	2021
NYC–Large Employers (of 11 or more)	$8.65/ 4.35	$10.00/ 5.00			
NYC–Small Employers (10 or less)	$8.00/ 4.00	$9.00/ 4.50	$10.00/ 5.00		
Long Island & Westchester	$7.50/ 3.50	$8.00/ 4.00	$8.65/ 4.35	$9.35/ 4.65	$10.00/ 5.00
Remainder of New York State	$7.50/ 2.90	$7.50/ 3.60	$7.85/ 3.95	$8.35/ 4.15	

Service Employees

The next schedule applies to other *service employees*. A service employee is one who is not a food service worker or fast food employee who customarily receives tips above an applicable tip threshold (which also follows schedules, not shown here).

Location	12/31/17	12/31/18	12/31/19	12/31/20	2021
NYC–Large Employers (of 11 or more)	$10.85/ 2.15	$12.50/ 2.50			
NYC–Small Employers (10 or less)	$10.00/ 2.00	$11.25/ 2.25	$12.50/ 2.50		
Long Island & Westchester	$9.15/ 1.85	$10.00/ 2.00	$10.85/ 2.15	$11.65/ 2.35	$12.50/ 2.50
Remainder of New York State	$8.65/ 1.75	$9.25/ 1.85	$9.85/ 1.95	$10.40/ 2.10	

Fast Food Minimum Wage

Non-exempt employees at some "fast food" restaurants are subject to an alternative minimum wage schedule.

The next schedule applies to employees who work in covered fast food restaurants whose job duties include at least one of the following: customer service, cooking, food or drink preparation, delivery, security, stocking supplies or equipment, cleaning, or routine maintenance.

These special New York minimum wage rates only apply to fast food restaurants that are part of a chain with at least 30 restaurants nationally.

Location	12/31/17	12/31/18	12/31/19	12/31/20	7/1/2021
New York City	$13.50	$15.00			
Outside of New York City	$11.75	$12.75	$13.75	$14.50	$15.00

Note: No tip credit is available for fast food employees.

Interns

There has been recent volatility regarding this question, especially under the federal FLSA. In 2010 the U.S. DOL issued guidance severely limiting for-profit companies' ability to have unpaid interns. However, courts routinely rejected the U.S. DOL's rigid six-part test. On January 5, 2018, the U.S. DOL modified its approach, adopting the "primary beneficiary" standard favored by the courts.

Which test applies and the resulting analysis determines whether a company violates the law by not paying interns minimum wage and overtime. It also affects other issues, such as coverage of employment discrimination laws; eligibility for unemployment, workers' compensation, disability, and other insurance benefits; and other protections/benefits afforded to employees, but not non-employees. (Because each law/agency applies somewhat different standards, we'll just focus on the basic question of minimum wage here, for threshold illustration purposes.)

"Primary Beneficiary" Test

This is the U.S. DOL's current test under the FLSA. Its seven factors are

1. The extent to which the intern and the employer clearly understand that there is no expectation of compensation. Any promise of compensation, express or implied, suggests that the intern is an employee—and vice versa.

2. The extent to which the internship provides training that would be similar to that which would be given in an educational environment, including the clinical and other hands-on training provided by educational institutions.

3. The extent to which the internship is tied to the intern's formal education program by integrated coursework or the receipt of academic credit.

4. The extent to which the internship accommodates the intern's academic commitments by corresponding to the academic calendar.

5. The extent to which the internship's duration is limited to the period in which the internship provides the intern with beneficial learning.

6. The extent to which the intern's work complements, rather than displaces, the work of paid employees while providing significant educational benefits to the intern.

7. The extent to which the intern and the employer understand that the internship is conducted without entitlement to a paid job at the conclusion of the internship.

The U.S. DOL emphasizes that "Courts have described the 'primary beneficiary test' as a flexible test, and no single factor is determinative. Accordingly, whether an intern or student is an employee under the FLSA necessarily depends on the unique circumstances of each case."

New York Department of Labor's Test

The U.S. DOL's position relates to whether an intern qualifies as an "employee" under the FLSA. It does not necessarily decide the question under other laws, including state minimum wage and overtime laws.

The NYS DOL uses both the six factors previously used by the U.S. DOL and five additional factors. In New York, an employer may have an unpaid intern where all of the following are true:

- The internship is similar to training received in an educational environment.

- The experience is for the benefit of the intern.

- The intern is not a substitute for regular employees and works under close supervision of existing staff.

- The employer derives no immediate advantage from the intern's activities.

- The intern is not guaranteed a job at the conclusion of the internship.

- Both the employer and the intern understand that the intern is not entitled to pay for the time spent in the internship.

- Any clinical training is performed under the supervision and direction of people who are knowledgeable and experienced in the activity.

- The trainees or students do not receive employee benefits.

- The training is general and qualifies trainees or students to work in any similar business. It is not designed specifically for a job with the employer that offers the program.

- The screening process for the internship program is not the same as for employment and does not appear to be for that purpose. The screening only uses criteria relevant for admission to an independent educational program.

- Advertisements, postings, or solicitations for the program clearly discuss education or training, rather than employment, although employers may indicate that qualified graduates may be considered for employment.

What Should Your Company Do About Unpaid Interns?

Despite relaxation at the federal level, the NYS DOL still applies a restrictive test for unpaid interns. (The above pertains to for-profit companies. Non-profits and governmental organization may have more leeway.)

Overall, for-profit employers (especially) should start by assuming that anyone working for them is an employee. They should only treat workers differently if there is a clear exclusion—e.g., valid intern or independent contractor.

Overtime

Most New York employers are subject to both federal and state minimum wage and overtime requirements. Usually, this means the employer must pay its employees at least the minimum wage for all hours worked and time-and-a-half for hours over 40 in a week. There are, however, many exceptions to these requirements.

Let's first look at how to calculate overtime (in the most typical scenarios). Then we'll turn to common exemptions.

Calculating the Overtime "Regular Rate"

The FLSA and New York overtime laws require employers to pay non-exempt employees overtime if they work enough hours (usually over 40/week). Overtime must be paid at one-and-a-half times the employee's "regular rate" of pay. (Employers can voluntarily agree to pay additional overtime premiums, but we're focusing on the statutory requirements.) Unfortunately, it's not always so easy to calculate the employee's regular rate.

Here we'll look at some of the most common regular rate calculation issues. I focus on calculations under the federal FLSA. New York follows the same basic rules, but there may be differences in non-routine situations.

Defining the "Regular Rate" of Pay

The FLSA's statutory definition of "regular rate" is very lengthy. The first few words define "regular rate" to include "all remuneration paid" to the employee. However, the next several hundred words identify exclusions.

More briefly stated than in the statute itself, these exclusions include certain:

- sums paid as gifts;
- payments made for occasional periods when no work is performed;
- reimbursements for traveling expenses;

- discretionary bonuses;

- profit sharing;

- payments made for employee benefits;

- additional compensation for hours worked beyond a specified number in a day/week or outside the normal workday/week;

- premium compensation for work on weekends or holidays; and

- income derived from qualifying stock transactions.

Many items above are more nuanced than described here. So, don't automatically exclude a payment just because it looks like it might fit on this list.

The "regular rate" is an hourly rate. It's always an hourly rate, even for employees not paid hourly. Many non-hourly employees are exempt, so it's unnecessary to calculate their regular rate. But some salaried employees are eligible for overtime. And some hourly employees also receive compensation beyond their base pay that counts toward their regular rate for overtime purpose.

When the Regular Rate Differs from the Base Hourly Rate

If a non-exempt employee receives any compensation other than their base hourly rate, the employer must consider what else to include in the regular rate when calculating overtime.

The regular hourly rate of pay of an employee is determined by dividing their total remuneration for employment (except statutory exclusions) in any workweek by the total number of hours worked in that workweek.

Let's look at how this work in several common situations.

Salaried Employees

If an employee's only form of compensation is a fixed salary per week, then you compute the regular rate by dividing the salary by the number of hours that the employer reasonably intends the salary to compensate. So, if the employee is paid $800 per week to work 40 hours, the regular rate is $20 per hour. If that employee works 50 hours in a week, then they would need to receive total pay of $1100 [$800 base salary for the first 40 hours and $300 ($20 x 1.5 x 10 hours) for the overtime].

Hourly Wage Plus Commissions

Some hourly employees are eligible to receive commissions or incentive bonuses based on a percentage of sales or another fixed formula. This additional compensation factors into the employee's regular rate for overtime calculations.

The calculation may be relatively straightforward where commissions are paid weekly. Then you just divide the commissions for the week by the number of hours worked in the week and add it to the base hourly rate earned in the week to determine the overtime regular rate. Take for example a non-exempt employee who works 45 hours with a $10/hour base rate. The employee also earns $90 in commissions for the week. Their regular rate in that workweek is $12 [the $10 base rate plus $2 ($90 in commissions / 45 hours worked)]. Their total compensation for the week, including overtime, must be $570 [$480 ($12 x 40 hours regular time pay, including commissions) + $90 (5 overtime hours x $12 regular rate, including commissions x 1.5)].

If, however, commissions are not earned and paid weekly, the calculation becomes more complicated. If the amount of commissions earned cannot be determined until after the regular payday for the workweek in which the employee performed the work that results in the commissions, then the commissions need not be included in the regular rate and paid as overtime on that payday. But, once determined, the commissions will eventually affect the regular rate and may require additional overtime calculations and payments. The U.S. Department of Labor has specific rules for calculating the regular rate and allocating the commissions over earlier workweeks to adequately compensate the employee for overtime earned.

Employees Working at Two or More Rates

Sometimes employees receive different rates of pay depending on what jobs or tasks they perform. By default, the regular rate is then determined by taking the weighted average of the separate rates earned. For example, the regular rate of an employee who spends 30 hours working for $15 and 20 hours working for $10 would be $13 per hour ($450 + $200 / 50). So the employee's total compensation would be $715 [$450 + $200 + $65 (the half-time portion of the 10 overtime hours, since the regular time portion is already included here)].

An employer may, however, have the option of instead paying overtime calculated at 1.5 times the rate for the specific work performed during the overtime hours. Using the previous example, had the employee worked all the overtime in the $10 job, then the regular rate for the overtime could be just the $10, rather than the weighted average wage. But the employee would have to apply this approach consistently. So, if the employee's overtime (i.e., the last hours worked in the week beyond 40) were in the higher paying job, then the regular rate would be $15 rather than $10. For the employer to use this approach, the employee must know of and be willing to work under this overtime structure before beginning the work.

The second method might be invalid if an employer uses it to systematically reduce an employee's overtime pay. This might be the case where the employer always requires the employee to perform the lower-rate work at the end of the week. Then the company may need to revert to the weighted average method.

Many More Regular Rate Scenarios Exist

These are just some of the most common methods for determining regular rate of pay for overtime purposes. The U.S. Department of Labor has permitted various other exceptions and approaches, either based on direct statutory instructions or as enforcement practicalities. Employers facing non-routine overtime issues should confer with experienced legal counsel. Mistakes in overtime calculations can lead to significant underpayment liability for employers, potentially including liquidated damages and attorneys' fees.

Exemptions

Both the FLSA and New York overtime laws recognize various exemptions, most prominently including the so-called "White Collar" exemptions. These exemptions only apply to employees whose actual job situations meet the requirements. Job titles do not automatically determine exemption, nor does the fact that the employee receives a salary.

The tests vary depending on the source of the requirement, but they are very similar. Because most New York companies must satisfy both state and federal law to avoid paying overtime, we'll separately identify the respective requirements.

Salary Threshold

As mentioned, receiving a salary does not automatically render an employee exempt from overtime. But receiving a sufficient salary is a component of many common exemptions.

One of 2016's hot topics in employment law was how high the salary threshold for FLSA exemption would increase? In other words, how much would employers have to pay exempt employees to keep them exempt? It's 2018, and the question hasn't gone away!

The U.S. Department of Labor initially answered it with a $913/week salary requirement. That threshold would have then changed every three years based on average salary levels. However, a federal court in Texas stopped the new salary rule before it took effect. That case remains on appeal, but the U.S. DOL—now under a different Presidential administration—has indicated it will not fight to uphold the $913/week standard. Instead, the U.S. DOL has announced that it will review the rules and establish a new test. In July 2017, the agency issued a Request for Information seeking information related to the FLSA exemption rules for the executive, administrative, professional, outside sales, and computer employee exemptions.

Like New York's minimum wage rates, the salary thresholds for New York's executive and administrative exemptions are established by schedules changing on December 31st of coming years. Notably, the New York thresholds are all higher than the existing FLSA threshold of $455/week. But, again, most New York companies must satisfy the higher New York threshold to ensure full overtime exemption.

There is no salary requirement for New York's professional or outside sales exemptions. But employers must also satisfy the $455/week FLSA threshold for most professional employees. However, there is no federal salary requirement to exempt doctors, lawyers, teachers, or outside salespersons.

Location	12/31/17	12/31/18	12/31/19	12/31/20	2021
NYC–Large Employers (11+ employees)	$975.00	$1,125.00			
NYC–Small Employers (<11 employees)	$900.00	$1,012.50	$1,125.00		
Long Island & Westchester	$825.00	$900.00	$975.00	$1,050.00	$1,125.00
Remainder of New York State	$780.00	$832.00	$885.00	$937.50	TBD*

Executive Exemptions

Despite the name, the "executive" exemption does not necessarily apply to all executives in a company. In fact, it often applies to employees who are not company executives.

FLSA

Under the FLSA, employees may be exempt under the executive exemption if:

1. They are compensated on a salary or fee basis of at least **$455** per week;

2. Their primary duty is the management of the enterprise or a customarily recognized department or subdivision of it;

3. They customarily and regularly direct the work of **two or more other employees**; and

4. They have the authority to hire or fire other employees or their suggestions and recommendations as to the hiring, firing, advancement, promotion, or any other change of status of other employees are given particular weight.

New York

Under New York law, employees can be exempt from minimum wage and overtime requirements if:

1. Their primary duties consist of management of the enterprise or a subdivision of it;

2. They customarily and regularly direct the work of **two or more other employees**;

3. They have the authority to hire, promote, advance, or fire other employees, or to effectively recommend such actions;

4. They customarily and regularly exercise discretionary powers; and

5. They receive **a sufficient weekly salary***.

*The weekly salary threshold now depends on geographic location within New York State. See the chart above to determine the applicable salary threshold.

Administrative Exemptions

Some areas in which employees eligible for the administrative exemption may work include finance, accounting, purchasing, marketing, research, human resources, IT, and legal. But not all employees in these areas are eligible for exemption.

FLSA

Despite the name, the "administrative" exemption does not necessarily apply to administrative assistants or certain other employees with "administrative" roles. In fact, it more often applies to director and executive level employees.

Under the FLSA, employees may be exempt under the administrative exemption if:

1. They are compensated on a salary or fee basis of at least **$455** per week;

2. Their primary duty is the performance of office or non-manual work directly related to the management or general business operations of the employer or the employer's customers; and

3. Their primary duty includes the exercise of discretion and independent judgment with respect to matters of significance.

New York

Under New York law, employees can be exempt from minimum wage and overtime requirements if:

1. Their primary duties consist of the performance of office or non-manual field work directly related to

management policies or general operations of the employer;

2. They customarily and regularly exercise discretion and independent judgment;

3. They regularly and directly assist the employer or an executive employee, or perform, under only general supervision, work along technical or specialized lines that requires special training, experience or knowledge; and

4. They receive **a sufficient weekly salary**.

Professional Exemptions

The professional exemptions only apply to certain employees in recognizable professional fields. Many other employees who probably consider themselves professionals will not qualify. However, such employees may be exempt under another exemption, such as the administrative or executive exemptions.

Of critical note, an employee does not automatically qualify for a professional exemption by having an advanced degree. The degree must qualify them in a professional field, and they must be performing the type of work typical to that profession.

Likewise, though often a critical element, a professional degree is not always necessary for the professional exemption. Extensive experience in a professional field can establish the required expertise in some cases.

FLSA

Under the FLSA, employees may be exempt as a "professional" if:

1. They are compensated on a salary or fee basis of at least **$455** per week, and;

2. Their primary duty is performing work that requires either:

    o   advanced knowledge in a field of science or learning customarily acquired by a prolonged course of specialized intellectual instruction ("learned professionals"), or

    o   invention, imagination, originality or talent in a recognized field of artistic or creative endeavor ("creative professionals").

The FLSA has a further special exception for specific categories of professional employees. There is no salary requirement for attorneys, medical doctors, and teachers working in those capacities.

To qualify for the professional exemption under the FLSA, other employees would have to receive the minimum salary. This includes engineers, architects, and artists, for example.

There is an additional potential FLSA exemption for certain computer employees. Employees performing jobs such as computer programming, software engineering, or systems analysis may be exempt even if they do not qualify for the professional exemption. The computer employee exemption also uniquely has an alternative hourly compensation threshold ($27.63 per hour) rather than only a salary threshold.

New York

Under New York law, employees can be exempt from minimum wage and overtime requirements if:

1. Their primary duties consist of the performance of work that either:

- requires knowledge of an advanced type in a field of science or learning customarily acquired by a prolonged course of specialized intellectual instruction and study (as distinguished from general academic instruction, an apprenticeship, or training in routine mental, manual, or physical processes); or

- is original and creative in character in a recognized field of artistic endeavor (as opposed to work which could be produced by a person endowed with general manual or intellectual ability and training), and the result of which depends primarily on the invention, imagination or talent of the employee.

  AND

2. The employee's work either involves the consistent exercise of discretion and judgment or is predominately intellectual and varied in character and is of the nature that the work produced cannot be standardized in relation to a given period of time.

Unlike the FLSA, New York law has no salary or fee basis requirement for professional employees. However, since most employees are subject to both the FLSA and state law, professional employees other than doctors, lawyers, and teachers may need to receive a sufficient salary to be exempt.

Outside Sales Exemption

Employers sometimes rely on the "outside sales" exemption to cover all categories of sales employees. But the "outside" component is critical for exemption. Sales employees who do not qualify under the outside sales exemption may still be eligible for another exemption, such as the executive or administrative exemptions.

In the past, this exemption covered more employees who went "door-to-door" or at least made home sales calls. Now, since most consumer purchases occur through the Internet, the exemption it is more prevalent among business-to-business sales employees.

But remember, the outside sales exemption only applies to employees whose actual job situations meet the requirements! Job titles do not automatically determine exemption, nor does the fact that the employee is involved in making sales.

FLSA

To qualify for the outside sales exemption under the FLSA:

1. The employee's primary duty must be making sales or obtaining orders or contracts for services or for the use of facilities for which a consideration will be paid by the client or customer; and

2. The employee must be customarily and regularly engaged away from the employer's place or places of business.

Unlike the administrative, executive, and professional exemptions, the FLSA salary requirements do not apply to the outside sales exemption.

An outside salesperson must travel to customers, usually at their places of business or homes. Selling solely by phone, mail, or the Internet does not qualify as outside sales.

"Sales" includes any sale, exchange, contract to sell, consignment for sales, shipment for sale, or other disposition. Promotional work related to the employee's own outside sales or solicitation efforts qualifies as exempt work.

New York

The FLSA and New York outside sales exemptions are very similar.

Under New York law, employees can be exempt from minimum wage and overtime requirements if they are customarily and predominantly engaged away from the premises of the employer and not at any fixed site and location for the purpose of:

- Making sales;

- Selling and delivering articles or goods; or

- Obtaining orders or contracts for service or the use of facilities.

Like the FLSA, New York has no salary requirement for outside sales employees. However, as discussed earlier, New York requires that *commissioned salespersons* have a written agreement establishing the terms of their compensation. (For outside sales employees whose primary compensation comes through a salary or hourly wage, employers still must satisfy the state's standard wage notice requirements.)

Exemptions Can "Expire"

Employers should periodically review employees' job duties to determine whether they qualify for an exemption. For example, employees who once supervised multiple employees, but now only oversee one, will no longer qualify for the executive exemption. But the administrative exemption, or another, might still apply.

In addition, employers must consider whether an employee's salary remains high enough to qualify for the exemption. Under New York law, the threshold is increasing annually, and at higher rates in some parts of the state. Remember that it is not enough to satisfy the federal salary threshold. When the New York threshold is higher, the employee would need to receive the higher salary level to be exempt (unless a different New York exemption applies).

Meal Period Requirements

The FLSA does not require employers to give their employees time off for lunch, dinner, etc. However, many states, including New York, impose meal period requirements.

Standard New York Meal Period

Every person employed in or in connection with a factory must be allowed at least an hour for the "noon day meal." If a factory employee works a shift of six or more hours that starts between 1:00 p.m. and 6:00 a.m., then they must also be allowed an hour meal period in the middle of the shift.

Employees other than those employed in or in connection with a factory must be allowed at least 30 minutes for the "noon day meal" if they work a shift of at least 6 hours that includes the hours from 11:00 a.m. to 2:00 p.m. If a non-factory employee works a shift of six or more hours that starts between 1:00 p.m. and 6:00 a.m., then they must be allowed a meal period of at least 45 minutes in the middle of the shift.

Additional Meal Period for All Employees

Any employee who works a shift that starts before 11:00 a.m. and ends after 7:00 p.m. must be allowed an additional meal period of at least 20 minutes between 5:00 and 7:00 p.m.

Exempt Employees Included

The New York meal period requirements apply to all employees, including those exempt from minimum wage and overtime.

One Employee Shift Exception

Usually, employees must be completely relieved from duty during the applicable meal periods. Accordingly, eating while working at one's desk does not count as taking a meal period. And the burden and obligation are on the employer to ensure that each employee receives the required meal period. Usually, the employee cannot consent to forego lunch.

However, in very limited situations where there is only one employee on duty, the NYS DOL may permit an employee to voluntarily agree to take their required meal period while still on duty. This exception is principally recognized in the retail context, where an employee may be able to sit and eat behind a sales counter mostly uninterrupted for much of the meal period. Even in these situations, an employee must be permitted to have a *completely* uninterrupted meal period upon request.

Shorter Meal Periods Permitted

As an enforcement matter, the NYS DOL permits any meal period to be shortened to no less than 30 minutes if there is no indication of hardship to employees.

The NYS DOL may allow shorter meal periods of not less than 20 minutes only in special or unusual cases. This exception requires an investigation by the NYS DOL and issuance of a special permit.

A New York Meal Period May Be Unpaid

The New York meal period law only requires that employees be relieved of duty to relax and eat. It does not require the employer to pay employees for that time. However, if, such as the case of the one employee shift exception, the employee is not entirely relieved from duty, they must be paid for the time even if they eat while working.

The New York meal period law does not require employers to give employees any further breaks during their shift. However, if employees take breaks of less than 20 minutes during their shift, that break time must be included as hours worked and paid accordingly.

Most companies should require hourly employees to "clock" in and out (by some method or another) before and after unpaid meal periods, but not around breaks (at least not for compensation purposes). It is always the employer's obligation to have accurate time records showing actual time worked, especially for non-exempt employees. In the event of an audit by the NYS DOL, it is also essential to show that employees receive the required New York meal periods.

Travel Time

Another complicated question is whether employers must pay for employee travel time.

What Is Work Time?

Most FLSA (and state law) compensation requirements are based on time worked. Work time is generally any time that an employer "suffers or permits" an employee to work.

Interestingly, the law doesn't tell us what "suffer or permit" means. But it's clear that time worked goes beyond time that the employer *intends* the employee to be working. It typically includes any time spent working on the employer's behalf, with or without permission.

What Isn't Work Time?

The FLSA does say something about what *doesn't* count as work time:

(1) walking, riding, or traveling to and from the actual place of performance of the principal activity or activities which such employee is employed to perform, and

(2) activities which are preliminary to or postliminary to said principal activity or activities,

which occur either prior to the time on any particular workday at which such employee commences, or subsequent to the time on any particular workday at which he ceases, such principal activity or activities. For purposes of this subsection, the use of an employer's vehicle for travel by an employee and activities performed by an employee which are incidental to the use of such vehicle for commuting shall not be considered part of the employee's principal activities if the use of such a vehicle for travel is within the normal commuting area for the employer's business or establishment and the use of the employer's vehicle is subject to an agreement on the part of the employer and the employee or representative of such employee.

What does all that mean in the context of travel time?

When You Do/Don't Have to Pay for Employee Travel Time

Standard commuting time to and from work usually is not work time. Travel during the work day as part of the employee's principal work activity is work time. However, things get more complicated if the employee travels out of town.

If an employee who normally works at one fixed location travels out of town and returns home the *same day*, then the extra travel time is work time. But the employer can subtract the usual commuting time.

Overnight out-of-town work travel adds another wrinkle. Then, the general rules are that:

1.Any time the employee spends actively working is work time (this includes travel time driving a car).

2. The portion of the day(s) when travel time crosses the employee's normal work hours is also work time (this includes time as a passenger).

The first of these rules is easy enough to follow/apply/accept. The second is harder. Consider the case of an employee who typically works 9:00 a.m. to 5:00 p.m. When she travels out of town for an overnight stay, the employer must count any travel time during those hours as work time, even if she isn't actively working or even driving. This even includes travel on days of the week that the employee doesn't usually work, such as weekends.

These rules pertain to minimum wage and overtime requirements for non-exempt employees. Employers do not have to pay exempt employees extra for their travel time absent an agreement to do so.

CHAPTER 3–PAID FAMILY LEAVE

As of January 1, 2018, non-governmental employers across the state of New York must allow their employees to take time off from work under the New York Paid Family Leave Program. Some of these businesses are already subject to the federal Family and Medical Leave Act (FMLA). However, the FMLA only covers employers with 50 or more employees and only permits *unpaid* leave. The New York *Paid* Family Leave Benefits Law applies to employers with as few as just one employee!

Although employers may pay for the insurance coverage themselves, the law was designed to be funded by employees through payroll deductions.

Which Employees Are Eligible?

For covered employers (virtually all non-governmental employers), employee eligibility for paid family leave depends on the employee's length of service.

Employees Whose Regular Schedule Is 20+ Hours Per Week

An employee who is regularly scheduled to work 20 or more hours per week becomes eligible once they have been employed for at least 26 consecutive work weeks.

There are special rules for employees working in businesses that regularly hire workers from day-to-day and where the nature of employment has breaks at certain times of year (e.g., schools).

Employees Whose Regular Schedule Is Less Than 20 Hours Per Week

An employee who is regularly scheduled to work less than 20 hours per week becomes eligible once they have worked 175 days for their employer.

Impact of Other Leaves in Determining Which Employees Are Eligible

In determining eligibility for paid family leave, using scheduled vacation, personal, sick, or other approved leave time is counted as consecutive work weeks or days worked if the contributions to the cost of family leave benefits have been paid for these periods of time.

However, periods of temporary disability taken under the New York Disability Benefits Law do not count. These include both short-term disability leaves and paid family leaves.

Family Leave Waivers

Certain employees unlikely to become eligible for paid family leave may file waivers to avoid contributing to the cost of paid family leave benefits.

An employee may waive coverage if:

- Their employment schedule is 20 hours or more per week, but they will not work 26 consecutive weeks; or

- Their regular work schedule is less than 20 hours per week, and they will not work 175 days in a 52-consecutive week period.

Employers must offer the waiver to employees eligible to waive coverage.

Employees who are eligible to file a waiver, but do not, must still contribute like other employees to the cost of paid family leave benefits through payroll deduction.

If the schedule of an employee who has filed a waiver changes, then their waiver may expire. This would occur within eight weeks of any change in their regular work schedule that requires the employee to work for 26 consecutive weeks or 175 days in a 52-consecutive week period. If this happens, then the employee becomes subject to payroll deductions. The deductions may begin even before the employee becomes eligible to take paid family leave.

When Can an Employee Take Paid Family Leave?

Now let's turn to the circumstances when an eligible employee may take leave.

Caring for a Family Member with a Serious Health Condition

Eligible employees may take leave to participate in providing care, including physical or psychological care, for a family member of the employee made necessary by a serious health condition of the family member.

Unlike the federal FMLA, New York's Paid Family Leave Benefits Law does not apply to an employee's *own* serious health condition.

Family Member

The following definitions apply for New York Paid Family Leave purposes:

- **"Family member"** means a child, parent, grandparent, grandchild, spouse, or domestic partner.

- **"Child"** means a biological, adopted, or foster son or daughter, a stepson or stepdaughter, a legal ward, a son or daughter of a domestic partner, or the person to whom the employee stands *in loco parentis.*

- **"Parent"** means a biological, foster, or adoptive parent, a parent-in-law, a stepparent, a legal guardian, or other person who stood *in loco parentis* to the employee when the employee was a child.

- **"Grandparent"** means a parent of the employee's parent.

- **"Grandchild"** means a child of the employee's child.

- **"Domestic partner"** includes a person at least 18 years of age (other than a close blood relative) who is dependent upon the employee for support as shown by either unilateral dependence or mutual interdependence, as evidenced by a nexus of factors including, but not limited to, common ownership of real or personal property, common householding, children in common, signs of intent to marry, shared budgeting, and the length of the personal relationship with the employee.

Serious Health Condition

"Serious health condition" means either:

- an illness, injury, impairment, or physical or mental condition that involves: inpatient care in a hospital, hospice, or residential health care facility; or

- continuing treatment or continuing supervision by a health care provider.

The Workers Compensation Board's Paid Family Leave regulations define the components of "serious health condition" in much more detail.

Bonding with a New Child

Eligible employees may take leave to bond with their child during the first 12 months **after** the child's birth or the placement of the child for adoption or foster care with the employee.

An employee may take paid family leave **before** the actual placement or adoption of a child if an absence from work is necessary for the placement for adoption or foster care to proceed.

An employee's right to take family leave for a birth expires at the end of the consecutive 52-week period beginning on the date of the birth.

An employee's right to take family leave for adoption or foster care expires at the end of the consecutive 52-week period beginning on the earlier of (1) the date of the placement or (2) the date of the first day of leave taken in connection with the placement.

Arising Out of a Qualifying Exigency Related to a Family Member's Active Military Duty

Eligible employees may take leave because of any qualifying exigency as interpreted under the FMLA, arising out of the fact that the spouse, domestic partner, child, or parent of the employee is on active duty (or has been notified of an impending call or order to active duty) in the armed forces of the United States.

The U.S. Department of Labor has identified nine categories of qualifying exigencies:

- Issues related to short-notice deployment;

- Attending military events and related activities;

- Certain childcare and related activities arising from the military member's covered active duty;

- Certain activities arising from the military member's covered active duty related to care of the military member's parent who is incapable of self-care;

- Making or updating financial and legal arrangements to address a military member's absence while on covered active duty;

- Attending counseling for the employee, the military member, or the child of the military member when the need for that counseling arises from the covered active duty;

- Taking up to 15 calendar days of leave to spend time with a military member who is on short-term, temporary Rest and Recuperation leave during deployment;

- Certain post-deployment activities within 90 days of the end of the military member's covered active duty; and

- Any other event that the employee and employer agree is a qualifying exigency.

Paid Family Leave Benefits

So, what benefits and protections are available to employees who take leave under the New York Paid Family Leave Program?

How Much Pay Do Employees Receive?

The amount of leave and pay available increases over the first few years of the New York Paid Family Leave Program. It starts at eight weeks and a maximum of 50% of the New York State Average Weekly Wage in 2018. It increases each year until reaching 12 weeks and 67% of the New York State Average Weekly Wage in 2021.

The following chart shows the number of weeks and percentage of weekly wage available each year.

Year	Weeks	Max % of Employee Average Weekly Wage	Capped at % of New York State Average Weekly Wage
2018	8	50%	50%
2019	10	55%	55%
2020	10	60%	60%
2021	12	67%	67%

Based on the 2017 New York State Average Weekly Wage of $1,305.92, the initial 2018 maximum paid family leave benefit was set at $652.96.

Employees' maximum paid family leave benefits may be limited by prior receipt of short-term disability benefits. The maximum combined benefit period for New York Paid Family Leave and short-term disability benefits is 26 weeks in any consecutive 52-week period. Thus, for example, if an employee has already received 20 weeks of disability benefits in the past year, they would only be eligible for up to 6 weeks of paid family leave.

Health Insurance Continuation

Group health insurance benefits provided to an employee before taking paid family leave must be maintained during paid family leave.

The employee remains responsible for any health insurance premium contributions during the paid family leave. Employers should make alternative arrangements to receive the contributions if they will not have paychecks to deduct them from during portions of the leave period.

Job Reinstatement

Covered employees who take paid family leave have the right to return to work at the end of the leave. The employee may be restored to either: the position the employee held when the leave began, or a comparable position with comparable employment benefits, pay, and other terms and conditions of employment.

If the employer refuses to reinstate the employee, the employee can file a "Request for Compliance." If the employer does not then reinstate the employee to the employee's satisfaction, the employee can file a complaint with the Workers' Compensation Board (WCB).

In evaluating an employee's complaint of failure to reinstate, the WCB "may consider whether the employer's actions are related to the taking of family leave or if the employer's actions would have affected the employee if he or she was not on family leave." For example, the WCB may consider whether the employee would have been laid off anyway for economic reasons.

Other employer defenses include that the employee was not eligible for paid family leave in the first place, or that the employee falsified their claim for benefits.

Other Paid Family Leave Benefits

Taking family leave also may not result in losing any employment benefit accrued before the leave began.

Additionally, the law protects employees from discrimination or retaliation for taking paid family leave. However, it does not entitle any restored employee to the accrual of any seniority or employment benefits during any period of leave, or any right, benefit, or position to which the employee would have been entitled had the employee not taken the leave.

Notice Requirements

The New York Paid Family Leave Benefits Law imposes notice requirements on both employers and employees. Failure to comply with these requirements can have serious consequences.

General Employer Notice Requirements

Covered employers must post a notice that the employer has secured insurance coverage for paid family leave benefits, as with workers' compensation insurance. The insurance carrier should supply this notice.

If the company maintains written employee guidance regarding benefits or leave rights, such as in an employee handbook, then the employer must include information about paid family leave.

An organization without an employee handbook must still provide written guidance to each employee about all of the employee's rights and obligations under the New York Paid Family Leave Benefits Law. The guidance must include information on how to file a claim for paid family leave.

Employee Notice Requirements

If the need for paid family leave is foreseeable, the employee must provide at least 30 days' notice before the leave will begin. Foreseeable events include an expected birth, placement for adoption or foster care, planned medical treatment, or a known military exigency.

If the leave is not foreseeable, then the employee need only provide as much notice as is practicable under the circumstances. According to the applicable regulations, "as soon as practicable" means "as soon as both possible and practical, taking into account all of the facts and circumstances in the individual case."

When an employee qualifies to take intermittent leave, the employer may require the employee to provide notice as soon as practicable before each day of intermittent leave.

In any case, employees need not give written notice to their employers. They also don't have to ask for paid family leave specifically. The employee need only provide enough information "to make the employer aware of the qualifying event and the anticipated timing and duration of the leave." The employer must ask for more information if necessary to determine whether the employee is seeking paid family leave.

Request for Paid Family Leave and Certification

Once the employer knows of the employee's potential leave, it must supply the employee with "Statement of Rights" and "Request for Paid Family Leave forms." As with a disability benefits claim form, the employer will complete a portion of the Request for Paid Family Leave. The employee will complete the rest, including providing the appropriate certification based on the nature of the leave.

The insurance carrier or third-party administrator will then process the Request for Paid Family Leave. Unless self-insured, the employer will not determine whether the claim qualifies for benefits or not. This differs from the federal FMLA, where the employer grants or denies the leave request.

Unfortunately, this creates a disconnect between the payment of leave benefits and the allowance of leave itself. The employer may have to, especially with unforeseeable leave, allow the employee to take time off before knowing whether the employee will ultimately receive benefits.

Disputes over eligibility for leave may result in arbitration between the employee and the insurance carrier or self-insured employers. Insured employers will not be parties to the arbitration, but may be directly affected by the outcome.

New York Paid Family Leave vs. FMLA

Especially for those who are already familiar with the federal FMLA, here's a summary of some of the differences under New York's Paid Family Leave Benefits Law. It's also a helpful synopsis even for employers not subject to the FMLA.

Covered Employers

FMLA: Governmental entities and private companies with 50 or more employees.

New York: All employers subject to the NY Workers' Compensation Law; but optional for governmental employers.

Eligible Employees

FMLA: Employed for 12 months and worked 1,250 hours in preceding 12 months; employer must have 50+ employees within 75-mile radius of the employee's worksite.

New York: Employed for 26 weeks (or 175 days if part-time).

Length of Leave

FMLA: Up to 12 weeks in a 12-month period.

New York: Up to 8 weeks in 2018; up to 10 weeks in 2019-2020; and up to 12 weeks beginning in 2021.

Leave Increments

FMLA: Employers must allow increments at least as small as one hour. If the employer allows shorter increments for other forms of leave, then the same shorter increments must also be available for FMLA leave.

New York: Employees can only take paid family leave in daily increments.

Compensation

FMLA: None required; may be able to use other available paid leave.

New York: 50% of Average Weekly Wages (AWW) in 2018; 55% of AWW in 2019; 60% of AWW in 2020; and 67% of AWW beginning in 2021.

Qualifying Circumstances

FMLA: New child (birth, adoption, foster); employee's own serious health condition; care for a family member with a serious health condition; "qualifying exigency" military leave; care for a military service member with serious injury or illness.

New York: Just new child, care for a family member with a serious health condition, and "qualifying exigency" military leave; **not** leave for the employee's own serious health condition.

Paid Time Off (PTO)

FMLA: Employers can **require** employees to use PTO (including vacation time, sick time, etc.) during FMLA leave.

New York: Employers have the option to **allow** employees to use PTO during paid family leave. If the employer gives the option, it's ultimately the employee's choice.

Administration

FMLA: All paperwork and decisions handled by employers.

New York: The Paid Family Leave Program is a component of employers' disability insurance policies and administered by the insurance carrier or self-insured employer.

CHAPTER 4–DISCRIMINATION

Many local, state, and federal laws prohibit employment discrimination across the United States. This chapter identifies different forms and aspects of discrimination law. All company executives, supervisors, and managers should be familiar with these concepts to provide the best opportunity to avoid claims. The next chapter goes into more detail on workplace harassment (a form of employment discrimination) and addresses what companies should do when complaints arise. While it is ideal to prevent discrimination before it occurs, how you handle complaints of employment discrimination can have a significant impact on your organization, for better or worse. Hopefully, by reading this book, it will be for the better!

What Laws Prohibit Employment Discrimination?

At the federal level, some of the key employment discrimination laws are:

- Title VII of the Civil Rights Act of 1964 (race, color, sex, national origin, religion)

- Americans with Disabilities Act (disability, perceived disability)

- Age Discrimination in Employment Act (age: 40+)

- Genetic Information Nondiscrimination Act (genetic information)

- Equal Pay Act (sex: compensation)

Across the state of New York, the New York Human Rights Law also provides protection based on:

- Age

- Color

- Creed

- Disability

- Domestic violence victim status

- Familial status

- Marital status

- Military status

- National origin

- Predisposing genetic characteristics

- Pregnancy-related condition

- Prior arrest or conviction record

- Race

- Sex

- Sexual orientation

For employees in the five boroughs of New York City, the New York City Human Rights Law also provides protection based on:

- Age

- Alienage or citizenship status

- Color

- Disability

- Gender (including sexual harassment)

- Gender identity

- Marital status and partnership status

- National origin

- Pregnancy

- Race

- Religion/Creed

- Sexual orientation

What Is Employment Discrimination?

Under the above laws, employment discrimination is an adverse impact based, at least in part, on a legally protected characteristic. Discrimination may occur regarding hiring, firing, promotion, compensation, or other terms and conditions of employment. Discrimination also includes harassment.

Unlawful harassment consists of unwelcome conduct that becomes a condition of continued employment and is severe or pervasive enough to create a work environment that a reasonable person would consider intimidating, hostile, or abusive.

The employment discrimination laws also prohibit retaliation for opposing unlawful discriminatory practices.

Employer Obligations under the ADA

Since 1990, the Americans with Disabilities Act (ADA) has protected individuals with disabilities. It applies to employers with at least 15 employees.

The ADA was amended in 2008 by the cleverly named Americans with Disabilities Act Amendments Act (yes, the ADAAA). The ADAAA did not change the definition of disability itself, but it expanded the scope of the components of the definition. As a result, the ADA now protects many more employees than it originally did.

The ADA prohibits discrimination against qualified individuals with a disability. It also requires employers to provide reasonable accommodations to employees with disabilities. Reasonable accommodations can range from time off from work to structural changes to the workplace.

So, which employees does the ADA protect?

An individual with a disability is a person who:

- Has a physical or mental impairment that substantially limits one or more major life activities;

- Has a record of such an impairment; or

- Is regarded as having such an impairment.

Let's break these down.

Physical or mental impairment that substantially limits one or more major life activities.

Physical or mental impairment:

(i) Any physiological disorder or condition, cosmetic disfigurement, or anatomical loss affecting one or more body systems, such as neurological, musculoskeletal, special sense organs, respiratory (including speech organs), cardiovascular, reproductive, digestive, genitourinary, immune, circulatory, hemic, lymphatic, skin, and endocrine; or

(ii) Any mental or psychological disorder, such as an intellectual disability, organic brain syndrome, emotional or mental illness, and specific learning disabilities.

Substantially limits:

This one is very complicated and discussed at length in regulations from the EEOC. Generally speaking:

An impairment is a disability if it substantially limits the ability of an individual to perform a major life activity as compared to most people in the general population. An impairment need not prevent, or significantly or severely restrict, the individual from performing a major life activity to be considered substantially limiting. Nonetheless, not every impairment will constitute a disability under the ADA.

Most notably, the regulations provide that:

> The term "substantially limits" shall be
> construed broadly in favor of expansive coverage,
> to the maximum extent permitted by the terms
> of the ADA. "Substantially limits" is not meant to
> be a demanding standard.

Major life activities:

Major life activities include, but are not limited to:

> (i) Caring for oneself, performing manual tasks,
> seeing, hearing, eating, sleeping, walking,
> standing, sitting, reaching, lifting, bending,
> speaking, breathing, learning, reading,
> concentrating, thinking, communicating,
> interacting with others, and working; and

> (ii) The operation of a major bodily function,
> including functions of the immune system,
> special sense organs and skin; normal cell
> growth; and digestive, genitourinary, bowel,
> bladder, neurological, brain, respiratory,
> circulatory, cardiovascular, endocrine, hemic,
> lymphatic, musculoskeletal, and reproductive
> functions. The operation of a major bodily
> function includes the operation of an individual
> organ within a body system.

Here again, the EEOC's regulations note that:

> The term "major" shall not be interpreted strictly
> to create a demanding standard for disability.
> Whether an activity is a "major life activity" is
> not determined by reference to whether it is of
> "central importance to daily life."

Record of such an impairment.

An individual has a record of a disability if the individual has a history of, or has been misclassified as having, a mental or physical impairment that substantially limits one or more major life activities.

Regarded as having such an impairment.

An individual is "regarded as having such an impairment" if the individual experiences a prohibited action because of an actual or perceived physical or mental impairment, whether or not that impairment substantially limits, or is perceived to substantially limit, a major life activity.

Prohibited actions include but are not limited to refusal to hire, demotion, placement on involuntary leave, termination, exclusion for failure to meet a qualification standard, harassment, or denial of any other term, condition, or privilege of employment.

Broader Coverage in New York

The New York State and New York City Human Rights Laws afford similar protections as the ADA to New York employees with disabilities. Under these laws, however, "disability" is defined much more broadly. Plus, they apply to employers with as few as four employees.

The New York State Human Rights Law defines "disability" as:

> (a) a physical, mental or medical impairment resulting from anatomical, physiological, genetic or neurological conditions which prevents the exercise of a normal bodily function or is

demonstrable by medically accepted clinical or laboratory diagnostic techniques or

(b) a record of such an impairment or

(c) a condition regarded by others as such an impairment.

The New York City Human Rights Law similarly defines "disability" as: "any physical, medical, mental or psychological impairment, or a history or record of such impairment."

These New York laws do not contain the same "substantial impairment" or "major life activity" conditions as the ADA.

Beyond not discriminating against employees with disabilities, covered employers must grant them work-related accommodations when necessary.

Reasonable Accommodations of Disability in Employment

Most business owners and managers know that employees with disabilities may be eligible for "reasonable accommodations." Fewer know where these obligations come from or precisely what they mean.

Job applicants also have rights regarding reasonable accommodations. These include accommodations to the hiring process as well as the position sought.

Applicable Laws

The ADA requires covered employers to provide reasonable accommodations to qualified individuals with disabilities.

The New York State and New York City Human Rights Laws also require covered employers to make reasonable accommodations.

Defining Reasonable Accommodation

Under the ADA, the EEOC has issued regulations defining reasonable accommodation to mean modifications or adjustments:

- to a job application process that enable a qualified applicant with a disability to be considered for the position the applicant desires;

- to the work environment, or to the manner or circumstances under which the position held or desired is customarily performed, that enable an individual with a disability who is qualified to perform the essential functions of that position; or

- that enable an employee with a disability to enjoy equal benefits and privileges of employment as are enjoyed by the employer's other similarly situated employees without disabilities.

The regulations further explain that accommodations may include:

- making existing facilities used by employees readily accessible to and usable by individuals with disabilities;

- job restructuring;

- part-time or modified work schedules;

- reassignment to a vacant position;

- acquisition or modifications of equipment or devices;

- appropriate adjustment or modifications of examinations, training materials, or policies;

- the provision of qualified readers or interpreters; and

- other similar accommodations for individuals with disabilities.

According to the U.S. Supreme Court, a modification or adjustment is "reasonable" if it "seems reasonable on its face," meaning the accommodation appears to be "feasible" or "plausible." It must also be effective in meeting the needs of the employee.

Under the New York State Human Rights Law, "reasonable accommodation" is defined similarly as:

> actions taken which permit an employee or prospective employee with a disability to perform in a reasonable manner the activities involved in the job or occupation sought or held and include, but are not limited to, provision of an accessible worksite, acquisition or modification of equipment, support services for persons with impaired hearing or vision, job restructuring and modified work schedules.

Undue Hardship

Even if an accommodation is "reasonable," the company does not have to provide it if it imposes an undue hardship on the business. Whether an accommodation would create an undue hardship must be determined case-by-case.

Undue hardship means a significant difficulty or expense in consideration of the:

- nature and net cost of the accommodation needed, taking into consideration the availability of tax credits and deductions, and/or outside funding;

- overall financial resources of the facility or facilities involved, the number of persons employed at the facility, and the effect on expenses and resources;

- overall financial resources of the employer, the overall size of the business of the employer with respect to the number of its employees, and the number, type, and location of its facilities;

- type of operation or operations of the employer, including the composition, structure, and functions of the workforce and the geographic separateness and administrative or fiscal relationship of the facility or facilities in question to the employer; and

- impact of the accommodation upon the operation of the facility, including the impact on the ability of other employees to perform their duties and the impact on the facility's ability to conduct business.

Similar factors and analyses of reasonable accommodations and undue hardship apply under the New York State and New York City Human Rights Laws.

Evaluating Accommodations

In seeking accommodation, the applicant or employee with a disability must let the employer know that they need an adjustment or change at work for a reason related to a medical condition. The person may use "plain English" and need not specifically mention any legal entitlement or use the phrase "reasonable accommodation."

Employees do not have a right to every accommodation they seek. Even if the employee's proposed accommodation is reasonable and does not impose an undue hardship, the employer may choose an alternative accommodation that meets the employee's needs.

When the availability or reasonableness of accommodations is in question, employers must engage in an "interactive process" with the employee. The EEOC suggests that the employer should give primary consideration to the employee's requested accommodation. However, the employer may provide the least expensive effective accommodation or the one that is the easiest to provide.

Limits on Reasonable Accommodations

It's often difficult to determine how far to go in accommodating an employee. But you can usually bear these limits in mind.

1. Performance standards regarding quality or quantity need not be lowered as a reasonable accommodation.

2. Jobs don't have to be restructured in a way that eliminates essential functions.

Preparing to Accommodate Disabilities

Companies should have policies and procedures in place for receiving and processing disability accommodation requests. Managers and supervisors must understand when an employee is requesting accommodation from them. Otherwise, they might unlawfully ignore a sufficient request. That can result in improper discipline or other undue consequence to the employee.

When management receives an accommodation request, it must not jump too quickly to conclusions about the feasibility of the request. Even expensive accommodations could be reasonable, and grants or other financial support may be available to defray the costs.

The United States Department of Labor's Office of Disability Employment Policy provides relevant services through the Job Accommodation Network (JAN). JAN provides information regarding available workplace accommodations to individuals and employers of all sizes.

Accommodating Religious Beliefs

Most U.S. employers are legally prohibited from discriminating in employment based on individuals' religious beliefs. Like with disabilities, but unlike most other employment discrimination protections, employers may need to accommodate employees' sincerely held religious beliefs.

Applicable Laws

Title VII prohibits employment discrimination because of race, color, religion, sex, or national origin. But only the religion component includes a reasonable accommodation requirement.

Title VII does not apply to *religious* organizations regarding the employment of individuals of a particular religion. Courts have limited this exception only to organizations whose "purpose and character are primarily religious." Even where this exemption applies, it only affects hiring and firing decisions. Once a religious organization hires employees of different religions, they cannot discriminate against them regarding pay, benefits, and other similar conditions of employment.

The New York State and City Human Rights Laws have similar requirements and exceptions.

Sincerely Held Religious Beliefs

Title VII defines religion to include "all aspects of religious observance and practice, as well as belief, unless an employer demonstrates that he is unable to reasonably accommodate to an employee's or prospective employee's religious observance or practice without undue hardship on the conduct of the employer's business."

The New York State Human Rights Law has different wording, but with similar impact:

> It shall be an unlawful discriminatory practice for any employer, or an employee or agent thereof, to impose upon a person as a condition of obtaining or retaining employment, including opportunities for promotion, advancement or transfers, any terms or conditions that would require such person to violate or forego a sincerely held practice of his or her religion, including but not limited to the observance of any particular day or days or any portion thereof as a sabbath or other holy day in accordance with the requirements of his or her religion, unless, after engaging in a bona fide effort, the employer demonstrates that it is unable to reasonably accommodate the employee's or prospective employee's sincerely held religious observance or practice without undue hardship on the conduct of the employer's business.

A religion does not have to be well-recognized or observed by many people to qualify an employee for Title VII protection. EEOC compliance guidance states that "religion" includes "religious beliefs that are new, uncommon, not part of a formal church or sect, only subscribed to by a small number of people, or that seem illogical or unreasonable to others." Religious beliefs can even include non-theistic beliefs.

No single rule determines whether an individual sincerely holds a religious belief. Some factors that might undermine asserted sincerity include whether the:

- employee has behaved markedly inconsistent with the professed belief;

- requested accommodation sought is a particularly desirable benefit that is likely to be sought for secular reasons;

- timing of the request is suspect; and

- employer otherwise has reason to believe the accommodation is not sought for religious reasons.

The requirement that a religious belief is "sincerely held" only applies regarding religious accommodations.

Religious Accommodations

Accommodations may include any adjustment to the work environment that will allow the employee to comply with their religious beliefs. Requests often relate to work schedules, dress and grooming rules, or religious expression or practice while at work.

The employee must initiate a request for accommodation by notifying the employer of the need for adjustment of work conditions due to a conflict with their religious beliefs. The employee must also explain the religious belief to the employer. The employer may seek additional information. But it cannot go so far as to discriminate against the employee by overly burdening them based on the request.

As with requests for accommodations based on disabilities, employees are only entitled to "reasonable accommodations" that do not impose "undue hardship" on their employer.

To show undue hardship in this context, the employer must identify (i) more than "*de minimis*" costs (under Title VII) or (ii) "significant expense or difficulty" (under the NYS and NYC laws) of providing the accommodation.

Both reasonableness and undue hardship are case-by-case determinations.

Handling Religious Accommodation Requests

Companies (through their managers) must be conscientious upon receiving a request for a change in work conditions related to religious beliefs. Ideally, there should be a procedure in place for receiving and processing these requests. Any sign of hostility toward a request may alone risk a claim of harassment or discrimination, even if no accommodation is due.

At the same time, employers need not automatically grant every request by an employee tied to a religious belief. Some may be unreasonable. Others may not be premised on a sincerely held religious belief. Still others may create an undue hardship. But all requests should be handled carefully so these criteria can be considered and appropriately weighed.

Association Discrimination

Most employers know they can't discriminate against employees based on the employees' own legally protected characteristics. But they may not realize that the same laws often also prohibit "association discrimination," or "relationship discrimination." In other words, employers can't discriminate based on an individual's association with someone in a protected class.

Forms of Association Discrimination

The employment discrimination laws don't always expressly identify what forms of association discrimination they prohibit. The courts have recognized forms of this protection by applying more general aspects of the laws.

An employee may be able to claim harassment or discrimination based on:

- a relative's disability;
- open association with or marriage to someone of a different race;
- being a parent or caregiver to children; and
- the protected activities of a relative.

Association Discrimination Under the ADA

The ADA is one law that contains express provisions about association discrimination. Among the forms of discrimination it prohibits is "excluding or otherwise denying equal jobs or benefits to a qualified individual because of the known disability of an individual with whom the qualified individual is known to have a relationship or association."

The ADA requires no familial relationship for an employee to receive this protection. The protection depends on whether the relationship of whatever type motivated the employer's action.

Association discrimination does not afford all of the same protections under the ADA as it does to an employee who has a disability. Most notably, employers do not have to provide accommodations to employees (or applicants) based on the disability of a relative.

Association Discrimination Based on Race

Unlike the ADA, Title VII does not contain any specific provisions about association or relationship discrimination. However, many courts have recognized such protections regarding race.

Here are some examples of actual cases where a court recognized a theory of racial association discrimination:

- A white man alleged he was fired because of his marriage to a black woman.
- A white woman alleged she lost her job because the employer disapproved or her social relationship with a black man.
- An employee alleged that his employer reacted adversely to him because his race differed from his daughter's.

Caregiver Discrimination

Title VII doesn't identify "caregivers" as a protected characteristic. But the EEOC and some courts have applied the law to provide employees rights to raise children.

Most of these cases have involved women claiming they were denied employment opportunities for having or wanting to have children. In a 2009 decision, one U.S. Court of Appeals (1st Circuit) summarized: "In the simplest terms, these cases stand for the proposition that unlawful sex discrimination occurs when an employer takes an adverse job action on the assumption that a woman, because she is a woman, will neglect her job responsibilities in favor of her presumed childcare responsibilities."

The EEOC has consistently taken this position, which it has described in assorted guidance documents.

Other Bases for Association Discrimination Claims

A few appellate courts have ruled that Title VII prohibits association discrimination regarding each of the law's protected characteristics. Most recently, the U.S. Court of Appeals for the Second Circuit (which covers New York as well as Connecticut and Vermont) ruled, "we now hold that the prohibition on association discrimination applies with equal force to all the classes protected by Title VII . . . ."

The Second Circuit made this pronouncement through a February 2018 decision in which the court ruled that Title VII prohibits sexual orientation discrimination through its general inclusion of sex as a protected characteristic. (The New York Human Rights Laws have long banned sexual orientation discrimination. But this ruling opens additional procedural options for employees claiming this form of discrimination. And additional remedies may be available to them under Title VII.)

Retaliation by Association

In 2011 the U.S. Supreme Court ruled that an employee may sue his employer for retaliation under Title VII claiming that he had been fired because his fiancée had filed a sex discrimination charge against their employer.

Before this decision, many courts had concluded that Title VII's retaliation protections only applied to the persons who personally engaged in protected activity. For example, the person who has filed a discrimination complaint. The Supreme Court, however, advised that "Title VII's antiretaliation provision prohibits any employer action that well might have dissuaded a reasonable worker from making or supporting a charge of discrimination."

On that standard, the Court continued: "We think it obvious that a reasonable worker might be dissuaded from engaging in protected activity if she knew that her fiance would be fired."

Employer Responsibilities

Many of the legal details in this area remain murky. The Supreme Court has not weighed in recently on most of these questions. It is not certain how it would rule in these cases today. Regardless, most employers don't want to be in the position of finding out directly. Accordingly, it is best to avoid any appearance of discrimination, whether based on an employee's characteristics or those of their relatives or others with whom they associate.

The next section discusses another somewhat related federal law, as it, among other things, prohibits discrimination in employment based on an individual's family medical history.

Genetic Information Protections

The federal Genetic Information Nondiscrimination Act (GINA) took effect in 2009. Today, most employers have still never heard of the law, which makes it illegal to discriminate against employees and applicants because of genetic information. Even those who have heard of GINA probably don't understand how extensive its protections are.

First, the law defines "genetic information" extremely broadly. It's not just the results of genetic tests.

Second, the law not only directly prohibits harassment and other discrimination, but also has strict rules against acquiring genetic information.

What Is Genetic Information?

"Genetic information" includes information about:

1. An individual's genetic tests;

2. The genetic tests of that individual's family members;

3. The manifestation of disease or disorder in family members of the individual (family medical history);

4. An individual's request for, or receipt of, genetic services, or the participation in clinical research that includes genetic services by the individual or a family member of the individual; or

5. The genetic information of a fetus carried by an individual or by a pregnant woman who is a family member of the individual and the genetic information of any embryo legally held by the individual or family member using an assisted reproductive technology.

Genetic information does not include information about the sex or age of the individual, the sex or age of family members, or information about the race or ethnicity of the individual or family members that is not derived from a genetic test.

GINA also defines "family member" broadly to include:

(1) A person who is a dependent of that individual as the result of marriage, birth, adoption, or placement for adoption; or

(2) A first-degree, second-degree, third-degree, or fourth-degree relative of the individual, or of a dependent of the individual.

In other words, "family member" includes the employee or applicant's parents, siblings, children, (great) (great-great) grandparents, (great) (great-great) grandchildren, (great) uncles, (great) aunts, nephews, nieces, first cousins, and first cousins once-removed. And it also includes all those relatives of the individual's dependents, which could include step-children and adopted children. Hence, an employee's genetic information could include information that has absolutely no genetic relationship to them personally!

GINA Prohibits Discrimination

GINA applies to all U.S. employers with 15 or more employees. It prohibits the use of genetic information in making employment decisions. This includes hiring, firing, promotions, compensation, and other terms and conditions of employment.

The law also prohibits harassment and retaliation related to genetic information.

Rules on Acquisition of Genetic Information

GINA also generally prohibits employers from requesting, requiring, or purchasing genetic information about applicants and employees.

These rules may be the biggest trap for the unwary under this law. While most employers aren't trying to discriminate based on genetic information (even as broadly defined here), they might be acquiring genetic information, especially family medical history.

For example, the EEOC's GINA regulations indicate that:

> "Request" includes conducting an Internet search on an individual in a way that is likely to result in a covered entity obtaining genetic information; actively listening to third-party conversations or searching an individual's personal effects for the purpose of obtaining

genetic information; and making requests for information about an individual's current health status in a way that is likely to result in a covered entity obtaining genetic information.

There are several exceptions to the rule against acquiring genetic information related to:

- Inadvertent requests;

- An employer's voluntary wellness program;

- FMLA certification;

- Acquisition through commercially and publicly available sources (e.g., newspapers, magazines, books);

- Monitoring the biological effects of toxic substances in the workplace; and

- Contamination testing by an employer conducting DNA analysis as a forensic laboratory.

These potential exceptions have nuanced parameters and require detailed analysis under the circumstances.

Of particular note, however, the EEOC regulations include specific safe-harbor language for requesting medical information about an employee from their medical providers. Using this language will protect a company regarding receipt of any medical information that the provider discloses:

> The Genetic Information Nondiscrimination Act of 2008 (GINA) prohibits employers and other entities covered by GINA Title II from requesting or requiring genetic information of an individual or family member of the individual, except as specifically allowed by this law. To comply with this law, we are asking that you not provide any genetic information when responding to this

request for medical information. 'Genetic information' as defined by GINA, includes an individual's family medical history, the results of an individual's or family member's genetic tests, the fact that an individual or an individual's family member sought or received genetic services, and genetic information of a fetus carried by an individual or an individual's family member or an embryo lawfully held by an individual or family member receiving assistive reproductive services.

GINA Confidentiality Requirements

GINA requires that employers maintain any genetic information they obtain about applicants and employees in medical files separate from personnel files and treat the information as a confidential medical record.

The ADA imposes similar confidentiality protections for an employee's own medical information.

New York Law

The New York State Human Rights Law bans discrimination based on "predisposing genetic information." This is defined as

any inherited gene or chromosome, or alteration thereof, and determined by a genetic test or inferred from information derived from an individual or family member that is scientifically or medically believed to predispose an individual or the offspring of that individual to a disease or disability, or to be associated with a statistically significant increased risk of development of a physical or mental disease or disability.

Under the Human Rights Law, New York employers generally may not:

(1) directly or indirectly solicit, require, or administer a genetic test to a person, or solicit or require information from which a predisposing genetic characteristic can be inferred as a condition of employment; or

(2) buy or otherwise acquire the results or interpretation of an individual's genetic test results or information from which a predisposing genetic characteristic can be inferred or to make an agreement with an individual to take a genetic test or provide genetic test results or such information.

Employee Off-Duty Conduct

In addition to the state and federal laws protecting employees based on inherent personal characteristics, New York law also prohibits discrimination against employees based on their lawful off-duty conduct. All New York employers are subject to these restrictions, regardless of size.

Protected Off-Duty Conduct

The New York Labor Law prohibits employers from discriminating against applicants and employees for any of the following:

1. Legal **political activities** outside of working hours, off of the employer's premises and without use of the employer's equipment or other property.

2. Legal **use of consumable products** before the beginning or after the conclusion of the employee's work hours, and off of the employer's premises and without use of the employer's equipment or other property.

3. Legal **recreational activities** outside work hours off of the employer's premises and without use of the employer's equipment or other property.

4. **Membership in a union** or any exercise of rights under the federal Labor Management Relations Act or New York's Taylor Law.

The law includes these specific definitions:

"**Political activities**" means "(i) running for public office, (ii) campaigning for a candidate for public office, or (iii) participating in fund-raising activities for the benefit of a candidate, political party or political advocacy group."

"**Recreational activities**" means "any lawful, leisure-time activity, for which the employee receives no compensation and which is generally engaged in for recreational purposes, including but not limited to sports, games, hobbies, exercise, reading and the viewing of television, movies and similar material." (Courts have ruled the law does not protect dating and romantic relationships as recreational activities, but that doesn't mean you should date your employees! See Chapter 1.)

"**Work hours**" means "all time, including paid and unpaid breaks and meal periods, that the employee is suffered, permitted or expected to be engaged in work, and all time the employee is actually engaged in work."

The law does not define "consumable products." However, the term includes legal tobacco products and alcohol.

Exceptions to These Protections

Like all good laws, there are exceptions to the above protections.

This law does not protect employees' off-duty conduct that creates a material conflict of interest related to the company's trade secrets, proprietary information, or other proprietary or business interest.

It also does not protect conduct by certain professional employees that violates: a collective bargaining agreement or a certified or licensed professional's contractual obligation to devote their entire compensated working hours to a single employer.

And a company does not violate this law where it acts based on the belief either that: (i) the employer's actions were required by law, (ii) the employer's actions were permissible under an established substance abuse or alcohol program or workplace policy, professional contract, or collective bargaining agreement, or (iii) the individual's actions were deemed by an employer or previous employer to be illegal or to constitute habitually poor performance, incompetency, or misconduct.

"Smokers' Rights"

The law intentionally permits employees to smoke tobacco outside of work. This prevents New York employers from having a policy of not hiring employees who smoke. However, the law does allow employers to impose higher insurance contributions on employees who smoke. It similarly allows employers to charge more for insurance based on dangerous recreational activities.

Some call this section of the New York Labor Law the "Smoker's Rights Law" or "bungee jumping law."

Consequences of Off-Duty Conduct Protections

This law has been in place for 25+ years. However, its importance may be increasing because of the proliferation of social media. As employees have more of their lives documented online, more companies see what their employees are doing outside of work.

Management does not always like what it sees. But much of the conduct reflected in social media posts could constitute use of consumable products or recreational activities.

Employers should be careful before acting based on such lawful off-duty activity. As mentioned, this law has many exceptions, but they are quite nuanced. In addition, various other employment laws may apply. It would be wise to consult with an experienced employment attorney before making employee decisions based on off-duty conduct.

Criminal Records

As with various categories of off-duty conduct, New York employers also cannot have blanket policies against hiring employees with criminal records. Instead, they must carefully consider several factors before using an applicant's criminal record to deny employment.

New York Corrections Law

The New York Corrections Law codifies the State's public policy supporting employment of people with criminal records. It provides that employers may not make negative employment decisions

> by reason of the individual's having been previously convicted of one or more criminal offenses, or by reason of a finding of lack of 'good moral character' when such finding is based upon the fact that the individual has previously been convicted of one or more criminal offenses, unless:
>
> (1) there is a direct relationship between one or more of the previous criminal offenses and the

specific employment sought or held by the individual; or

(2) the granting or continuation of the employment would involve an unreasonable risk to property or to the safety or welfare of specific individuals or the general public.

This law only applies to prior convictions. It does not apply to convictions occurring during employment with the employer in question.

The law identifies eight factors that employers must consider in deciding whether a criminal conviction disqualifies an individual from employment in a particular position:

1. New York's public policy encouraging the employment of persons previously convicted of one or more criminal offenses.

2. The specific duties and responsibilities necessarily related to the employment sought or held by the person.

3. The bearing, if any, the criminal offense or offenses for which the person was previously convicted will have on the person's fitness or ability to perform one or more of the job's duties or responsibilities.

4. The time elapsed since the criminal offense or offenses.

5. The age of the person at the time of the criminal offense or offenses.

6. The seriousness of the offense or offenses.

7. Any information produced by the person, or produced on his behalf, regarding their rehabilitation and good conduct.

8. The legitimate interest of the employer in protecting property and the safety and welfare of specific individuals or the general public.

Notice to Applicants

If a job candidate with a criminal record asks an employer for a statement of the reasons they were denied employment, then the employer must provide one in writing within 30 days.

Employers who learn of criminal records through background checks must satisfy additional notice requirements under fair credit reporting laws.

New York Human Rights Law

An employee with a criminal record can claim discrimination on this basis under the New York State Human Rights Law, which specifically references violation of the Corrections Law provisions above as violating the Human Rights Law.

As a result, applicants and employees can file claims of criminal record discrimination like other employment discrimination claims in New York. This means they can file a complaint with the New York State Division of Human Rights or directly with a court.

The New York City Human Rights Law also has similar provisions.

How to Stay Out of Trouble

These laws do not say that employers can't use criminal records as part of their employment decisions. Rather, they mean that employers must evaluate each situation individually.

Companies should document their consideration of all the factors listed above any time they deny employment based on a prior criminal conviction. This documentation alone should improve your defense of a criminal record discrimination claim. Businesses who can't show they weighed the statutory factors may not be able to overcome that failure.

Remember that the overriding question is how closely related the convictions are to the jobs in question. Banks probably need not hire former bank robbers. But clothing stores probably can't turn down applicants because of their misdemeanor public intoxication charges from college.

Ban-the-Box Laws

Although the New York State Human Rights Law restricts inquiries about criminal records to some degree, it has historically been permissible to at least ask whether the applicant has ever been convicted of a felony on job applications. In recent years, however, some New York cities have adopted local laws restricting this practice.

"Ban-the-box" laws get their name because they literally prohibit employers from including a check box (or other item) on job applications asking whether the applicant has a prior criminal record. New York still does not have a statewide ban-the-box law, but Buffalo, Rochester, and New York City (the three largest cities in the state) have now implemented these laws through local ordinances. If you are hiring in or do business with these cities, then you need to double check your employment applications to make sure your organization is complying.

Buffalo's Ban-the-Box Law

The City of Buffalo passed a ban-the-box law in 2013 that took effect in 2014. This law applies to employers located within the City of Buffalo, as well as any vendors of the City of Buffalo (regardless of their location), with 15 or more employees. The law prohibits these covered employers from asking about criminal convictions on job applications and any time before the first job interview.

Job applicants may sue employers directly for violating this law. If they prevail, applicants can recover injunctive relief, damages, and attorneys' fees.

Anyone can also file a complaint with the Buffalo Commission on Citizens' Rights and Community Relations. This Commission can cause the City of Buffalo's Corporation Counsel to pursue a claim against an employer in violation of the ban-the-box law. Penalties include $500 for the first violation and $1,000 for each subsequent violation.

There are exceptions to the Buffalo ban-the-box law for situations where criminal convictions would legally restrict the ability of the applicant to perform the job.

Rochester's Ban-the-Box Law

Rochester also imposed a ban-the-box law in 2014. It applies to all employers (public and private) and employment agencies with four or more employees that employ individuals within the City of Rochester. It also applies to any vendors, contractors, or suppliers of services or materials to the City of Rochester (regardless of their location).

Like the Buffalo law, Rochester's ban-the-box law allows applicants to sue employers directly for injunctive relief, damages, and attorneys' fees. Also like the Buffalo ban-the-box law, Rochester's law permits the City's Corporation Counsel to bring legal action to recover civil penalties of $500 for the first violation and $1,000 for each subsequent violation.

The Rochester ban-the-box law also has exceptions. For example, it allows inquiries where the conviction would legally prohibit someone from working in the position.

New York City's Ban-the-Box Law

The New York City Fair Chance Act took effect in October 2015. It prohibits employers with four or more employees from asking about an applicant's pending arrest or criminal conviction record until after the employer has made a conditional offer of employment. Under this law, employers are further prohibited from even searching publicly available sources to obtain information about an applicant's criminal history before making a conditional offer of employment.

Again, there are exceptions where a law requires a background check for a job or a criminal conviction would legally bar the applicant from taking the position.

When Should I Ask About Criminal Records?

Employers in cities with ban-the-box laws may not initially ask about criminal convictions, unless the information is related to specific job criteria imposed by law. Moreover, even where there is no ban-the-box law in place, New York companies should be careful with obtaining and considering criminal record information in making employment decisions.

First, before obtaining a background check from a third-party service, an employer must obtain written authorization from the applicant and satisfy other requirements of the Fair Credit Reporting Acts.

Second, a company that obtains any information about prior criminal records, either from the applicant directly or through other sources, must carefully consider whether the conviction(s) should disqualify the candidate for employment.

Third, given the above considerations, many employers would be well-advised not to seek any information about a job candidate's criminal history until after making a conditional offer of employment. This will help protect against claims of criminal record discrimination in cases where the applicant would not have been hired anyway based on other criteria. It will also limit the instances where background checks need to be obtained and the multi-factored analysis described above must be conducted.

USERRA Reinstatement Rights

Before we move on to the discussion of harassment, I want to address one special component of the federal military employee rights law. In addition to generally prohibiting discrimination based on military service, the Uniformed Services Employment and Reemployment Rights Act of 1994 (USERRA) affords employees rights to return to work following certain military leaves. These reinstatement rights include an "escalator principle" unique among employee leave protections.

USERRA Coverage

USERRA applies to all U.S. employers of any size. Its military leave and reemployment provisions apply to all employees absent from work because of service in the uniformed services. However, per federal regulations, it does not cover: "Employees whose employment before military service was for a brief, non-recurrent period, when there was no reasonable expectation the employment would have continued indefinitely or for a significant period."

Under USERRA, "uniformed service" includes

1. **Armed forces**, including:

- Army and Army Reserve;

- Navy and Naval Reserve;

- Air Force and Air Force Reserve;

- Marine Corps and Marine Corps Reserve; and

- Coast Guard and Coast Guard Reserve.

2. **National Guard**, which includes the Army National Guard and the Air National Guard, when the service member is engaged in:

- active duty for training;

- inactive duty training; or

- full-time National Guard duty.

3. **Commissioned Corps of the Public Health Service.**

4. **Any other category of persons designated by the President in time of war or national emergency.**

"Service" in the uniformed services includes

- Active duty;

- Active duty for training;

- Initial active duty for training;

- Inactive duty training;

- Full-time National Guard duty;

- Submitting to an examination to determine an individual's fitness for these services;

- Funeral honors duty performed by National Guard or Reserve members;

- Duty performed by intermittent disaster response personnel for the Public Health Service and approved training to prepare for this service; and

- Service as an intermittent disaster response appointee of the National Disaster Medical System when participants are activated under federal authority or attending authorized training to support their federal mission.

Notice of Military Service

USERRA only provides leave protections to employees whose employers received advance notice of the employees' intent to take military leave.

Either the employee or an authorized military officer may provide the notice. The notice need not be formal or in writing. Often, however, employers obtain copies of military orders or training notices.

The Department of Defense encourages that the employer receive notice at least 30 days before the leave starts. But no specific notice period is required.

No advance notice is required if it cannot be given because of military necessity or it is impossible or unreasonable to give advance notice.

Reemployment Rights

Employers must reemploy an employee who was on leave for service in the uniformed service where the:

- Employer received advance notice of the military service;

- Employee's cumulative military service does not exceed 5 years during employment with the employer (with some exceptions);

- Employee returns to work or seeks reemployment promptly; and

- Employee was not separated from the uniformed service for a disqualifying reason.

Timely Return to Work

The time within which employees must return to work following military leave depends on the length of their leave, as follows.

- **Less than 31 days:** Employee must report to work at the beginning of the first regularly scheduled workday starting at least eight hours after they return home.
- **31 to 180 days:** Employee must apply for reinstatement within 14 days after completing military service.
- **More than 180 days:** Employee must apply for reinstatement within 90 days after completing military service.

Employees may have additional time where circumstances make it impossible to return to work in the stated time periods. For example, injured service members may have up to two years or more to return to work following military service.

Employees do not automatically lose reinstatement rights if they do not report back to work within the applicable time periods. Rather, they would then become subject to the employer's rules about unexcused absences.

Employers must reinstate qualifying employees within two weeks (or sometimes less), barring unusual circumstances.

"Escalator Principle"

Laws that require employers to reinstate employees following leave (like the FMLA) usually only require reinstatement to the same or comparable position. USERRA is different. It requires employers to reemploy service members *in the position they would have attained* had they not been absent for military service. The employee must receive the same seniority, status, pay, rights, and benefits they would have achieved but for the military leave.

This "Escalator Principle" applies even if it requires the company to bump another employee, train the returning service member, or find another comparable position if the "escalator" position no longer exists. In the latter situation, the employer's obligation depends on the length of the military service, whether the employee is disabled, and the employee's qualifications.

Changed Circumstances and "Undue Hardship"

Employers do not always have to reinstate employees following covered military leaves.

This includes situations where the employer's circumstances have changed such that reemployment would be impossible or unreasonable. For example, a company that has conducted a reduction in force that would have included the employee may not have to reinstate the employee just because she was on military duty.

Employers likewise do not have to train or retrain returning service members to qualify them for reemployment if it would cause an undue hardship.

Action otherwise required under USERRA creates an undue hardship if it requires significant difficulty or expense. The analysis involves many factors, such as overall financial resources of the employer and cost of the required action.

Protection from Termination

An employer may not terminate a reinstated employee whose military service lasted more than 30 days "without cause" for a period of:

- 180 days, if the military service lasted 31 to 180 days, or

- One year, if the military service lasted 181+ days.

"Cause" may exist based on misconduct or other legitimate nondiscriminatory reasons.

USERRA's general anti-discrimination principles still protect employees whose military service lasted less than 30 days from discrimination based on their military service. But the employer does not have the initial burden to prove "cause" in that scenario.

CHAPTER 5-HARASSMENT

Most employers do—and all should—have written policies regarding workplace harassment. These policies don't exist just for legal reasons. Harassment is bad in itself, plus it interferes with productivity. But not all harassing behavior violates employment discrimination laws.

"Harassment" is a broad term. It could include simply being obnoxious, which isn't necessarily illegal. But when talking about workplace harassment, we typically mean unwelcome conduct related to a legally protected characteristic. It's not just sexual harassment. Discrimination laws prohibit harassment based on numerous characteristics. Age, race, disability, and religion are just a few of the most prevalent.

No workplace with more than a few employees can simply rest assured that these topics won't come up in ways that make employees uncomfortable. You must be proactive both to prevent harassment in the first place and to stop it before it escalates. Even if managers themselves avoid doing or saying inappropriate things, they must keep other employees in line.

All Harassment Is Bad for Business

Not all harassment that occurs at work violates employment discrimination laws. But virtually all workplace harassment has negative consequences. If nothing else, it makes the victim of harassment less comfortable in their job. That usually hurts productivity. Lower productivity creates plenty of problems, including lower overall morale. Reduced worker morale also leads to higher absenteeism and even lower productivity. Eventually this can mean lower revenue. Loss of profits can necessitate layoffs. . . .

And all that can occur if only one employee perceived harassment just once! Never mind that the employee may tell a co-worker, who may also become uncomfortable. The second employee's discomfort can be because they also feel offended by what the "harasser" did. Or just because they feel bad for their co-worker. Or because they don't know whether they should tell someone else, etc.

As the story spreads—potentially with some details morphing in various directions—many employees become involved. And the impacts on the organization multiply.

Unlawful Workplace Harassment

Harassment becomes unlawful where:

1. enduring the offensive conduct becomes a condition of continued employment, or

2. the conduct is severe or pervasive enough to create a work environment that a reasonable person would consider intimidating, hostile, or abusive.

The "reasonable person" standard means that it's not enough that the specific employee involved feels this way. If most similarly situated people would not be offended, then the conduct wouldn't rise to the level of being unlawful. Again, that doesn't mean it is acceptable in the workplace.

Forms of Harassment

Harassment can come in numerous forms, including:

- offensive jokes;
- slurs;
- epithets or name calling;
- physical assaults or threats;
- intimidation, ridicule or mockery;
- insults or put-downs;
- offensive objects or pictures; and
- interference with work performance.

In addition, the anti-discrimination laws protect employees from workplace harassment not only by co-workers and supervisors, but also by third parties. Thus, companies must prevent and remedy inappropriate conduct by vendors, customers, visitors, contractors, etc., against their employees. If employers permit harassment by outsiders to persist to the point of unlawful harassment, then the employer may be legally responsible.

How to Avoid Unlawful Harassment?

The best way to avoid *unlawful* harassment is to prevent harassment altogether. This is why employers should have anti-harassment policies that go beyond just what the law prohibits. Don't tolerate behavior that even comes close to the line.

In addition to a well-written and carefully followed policy, companies should also train employees about harassment. Many employers include anti-harassment training in their on-boarding process. But it is a good idea to also provide periodic group training to all employees. Several states require private companies to do so. New York has not yet, but probably will soon.

Finally, employers must respond promptly to all complaints of workplace harassment. Investigating thoroughly and taking appropriate action will hopefully avoid escalation. If not, the company's good faith attempts to keep the workplace free of harassment may still help avoid liability.

Managers' Role

Managers have many duties. But, generally, a primary function is to keep other employees productive. Hence, they can't tolerate harassment and its potentially disastrous implications.

Yes, it's a given that managers must understand what harassment is and refrain from engaging in it. They should set the example for others. This alone is easier said than done.

Beyond that, all managers must be attentive to what other employees are doing and respond when someone crosses the line. They can't hear something inappropriate and just write it off as an innocent joke. If there is any indication that the conduct may have offended someone, then the manager must step in, at least to report it to the appropriate personnel so they can investigate.

Similarly, when employees report incidents of possible harassment to managers, the managers can't just handle it themselves. They must involve others as appropriate, consistent with the organization's anti-harassment policy. Usually, the company will need to investigate carefully, and the first manager to hear of an incident may not be the right one to do that.

Besides the effects on morale and productivity, there are legal consequences when managers don't do the right things.

Employer Liability

Companies are strictly liable when an owner or high-level manager commits unlawful harassment. In these cases, the employer can argue that no harassment occurred. But it probably won't avoid liability by proving that the victim didn't report the harassment.

Employers may also be automatically liable for harassment by lower-level managers and supervisors with sufficient control over the working conditions of the victim.

When co-workers or lower-level managers with no direct control over the victim's working conditions engage in harassment, their employers are not necessarily responsible. In these cases, the company's legal obligation usually kicks in only when it (through higher level managers) knew or should have known about the harassment.

Manager Liability

The New York State Human Rights Law, unlike Title VII, directly holds some managers accountable for harassment (and other forms of employment discrimination). It permits individual liability for both employees who commit harassment and supervisors who ignore their duty to investigate and remedy it.

Although plaintiffs usually file discrimination complaints against the company itself, they sometimes also name individual employees as defendants. Depending on the circumstances, the employer might or might not pay for the manager's legal defense or any settlement or verdict against them.

Penalties

Employees have up to three years to file sexual harassment claims in New York. Under the State Human Rights Law, an aggrieved employee can recover lost wages and benefits (backpay and frontpay), emotional distress, and compensatory damages. Unlike Title VII, the Human Rights Law does not cap potential emotional distress damages. However, the Human Rights Law does not provide for punitive damages like Title VII does.

Generally, attorneys' fees are not available under the Human Rights Law's employment provisions. However, recent amendments now permit the prevailing party to obtain an attorney's fee award in sex discrimination cases only. This includes New York sexual harassment cases.

Sexual Harassment

Sexual harassment is a hot topic in the media these days. It warrants attention from many angles and stakeholders. I'm focusing on the workplace here. But, of course, sexual harassment, assault, and abuse also affect many other aspects of our lives.

Sexual Harassment: The Laws

Title VII prohibits discrimination in employment because of sex (among other characteristics). Harassment is a form of discrimination. Thus, Title VII prohibits sexual harassment in the workplace, as do the New York State and New York City Human Rights Laws.

The New York State Human Rights Law prohibits sexual harassment in all workplaces across the state. The law also bans other forms of discrimination and harassment by employers with at least four employees. But in 2015, the law was amended to extend the protection against sexual harassment to all employers *of any size*. (Remember, Title VII only applies to employers with at least 15 employees.)

What Is "Sex"?

New York's sexual harassment law may also be broader than federal laws, as state regulations now expressly define the term "sex" to include gender identity and the status of being transgender.

Indeed, the state regulations expressly provide that "Harassment on the basis of a person's gender identity or the status of being transgender is sexual harassment."

Forms of Sexual Harassment

Under the Human Rights Law and Title VII, there are two forms of sexual harassment:

"Hostile work environment" harassment consists of comments, acts, conduct, behavior, etc., of intimidation, humiliation, or ridicule of a sexual nature or based on an individual's sex.

"Quid pro quo" harassment involves a request for sexual activity in exchange for favorable job treatment. Whereas a hostile work environment can exist based on any protected characteristics (e.g., race, religion, age), quid pro quo harassment can only apply to sexual harassment.

Sexual assault (usually involving physical contact) is also illegal, of course. It can be both a criminal offense and a civil one (a tort). Beyond employment discrimination laws, employers could, in some cases, be held legally culpable for enabling, permitting, tolerating, etc., sexual assault.

More Than a Legal Problem

The recent media attention on sexual harassment and assault identifies some high-profile perpetrators. They may be celebrities. They may be wealthy. Regardless, they usually have jobs (or run their own businesses).

Sexual harassment and assault are wrong in themselves and in a million ways. But let's just consider the employment context. What are some negative impacts?

Let's face it, sexual harassment isn't good for morale. Even unintentional, relatively minor instances can permeate the workplace. They may only upset one employee. Or one employee can tell another, and people get uncomfortable. An otherwise respected boss or co-worker falls out of favor (probably rightly so, though some are occasionally falsely accused).

Unfortunately, not all cases of sexual harassment are reported to human resources or others in the organization that could hopefully do something about it. But the ones that are reported demand action. Action requires resources (time, money, etc.) that companies would rather be able to spend elsewhere. We can't blame this on the victims. The blame is on those behaving inappropriately. But we can all agree it would be better if there were no harassment to be investigated in the first place.

What's the Fix?

Sexual harassment is wrong, and it's bad. That doesn't mean it's easy to cure. But it also doesn't mean we shouldn't try.

Briefly, here are some basic elements every employer should implement:

- Anti-harassment policy;
- Training all employees;
- Additional training for supervisors;
- Effective complaint procedures;
- Designated compliance officers;
- Prompt investigations; and
- Effective remedial action.

Additional steps may be appropriate in some companies. These could include, for example, conducting workplace satisfaction surveys, expanding the human resources team, and other initiatives to promote pervasive professionalism.

Don't Ignore It

I hope the recent public disclosures and related dialogue about this subject will help reduce sexual harassment. But no one should assume it can't happen to them or in their organization.

Management teams must take the lead to put out any flames before they spread. The financial motivation itself is real. Some legal settlements have recently been reported to reach the range of $32 million to a single victim. Most employers would not survive that loss, or even anything close. The public relations backlash could be even worse.

But, most important, people must live with themselves and sleep at night. That alone is reason enough not tolerate harassment on our watch.

Avoiding Liability

The best approach is to take reasonable precautions and prevent harassment before it happens. This primarily occurs through training of all employees, including supervisors.

But employers do not always have perfect control over what their employees do. So, when there is concern that someone has crossed a line, the company must act prudently to ensure that the behavior stops. The first step to accomplishing this is having an effective complaint procedure. The second step is investigating all complaints thoroughly. The third step is taking appropriate remedial action based on the investigation.

Be Prepared

No company wants to deal with allegations of sexual harassment. But even the best-run organizations must be proactive to avoid it. This includes having a well-written anti-harassment policy and conducting periodic training. It also includes being ready to investigate promptly and effectively. Individuals responsible for investigating sexual harassment should obtain additional training in that area.

How Should Managers Be Held Accountable?

We often speak of the *company* being liable for harassment and discrimination. But, there's never any violation of law without *people* acting or failing to act. Every organization (through its people) must hold its people (particularly management) accountable for avoiding employment discrimination. In broad strokes, here's how:

First, position them for success. Employers should provide training for all managers on harassment, including their heightened responsibilities in dealing with it.

Second, monitor managers' performance in this area. If nothing else, pay attention when complaints come forward. Determine which managers knew or should have known something sooner. Investigate that in addition to the incident of harassment.

Third, discipline when warranted. Remember all the potential costs of harassment to the company? It can't afford bear those repeatedly. If a manager put the business at risk by not handling a harassment situation properly, that can't be ignored. Sometimes retraining the manager may suffice. In more egregious situations formal discipline up to termination may be in the company's best interest, even if the manager brings a lot to the table in other areas.

Fourth, hire the right managers. Arguably, this could be the first step. But few employers will start out by focusing on hiring people who are good at freeing a workplace of harassment. That can change, though, after a couple bad situations come to light. Remember that just because someone is great at making widgets, it doesn't mean they will make a great widget manager. It's more likely that a great manager can succeed in the role even if they don't personally know how to make the widgets. As long as they can keep the people who are skilled at making widgets in line, the business can be productive.

Anti-Harassment Policies

It's not just sexual harassment. Workplaces should be free of harassment based on all the other protected characteristics as well. This includes racial harassment, age-based harassment, harassment of individuals with disabilities, etc.

Every organization should have a written anti-harassment policy. These policies should prohibit harassment based on all legally protected characteristics. These usually include sex, race, age, disability, and religion, among others. I suggest that most employers have "zero tolerance" for violations of these policies. But what does that mean?

What Is Zero Tolerance?

I have written and reviewed anti-harassment policies for over a decade. I have even argued over them in court. You may be surprised that I've probably spent more time defending companies for firing employees who violated these policies than I have spent defending employers against claims of harassment itself! It turns out that employees don't always accept that they've harassed someone, or at least, they don't accept the consequences.

Anyway, over the years I've realized that many people don't understand what the "zero-tolerance" provision of their anti-harassment policy means. They think it means they must fire anyone who violates the policy. But that's not what it should mean.

You can have "zero tolerance" without automatically removing every offender from the workplace. But you must take harassment seriously and address every violation of the policy appropriately.

Whom Does the Policy Cover?

In part, zero tolerance means the policy covers everyone.

This includes everyone in the organization, regardless of title, responsibility, performance, etc., all the way up to the CEO and owners. It also includes third parties who interact with the company: contractors, vendors, customers, clients, etc. No one is important enough to be immune.

No one should be harassing your employees. If they are, do something about it!

Zero-Tolerance Responses

Good employers also demonstrate zero tolerance by taking meaningful action when they decide someone has harassed an employee. They don't decline to act just because the harassment isn't illegal.

The anti-harassment policy should identify who is responsible for enforcing it and to whom employees should report harassment. Once management knows of a harassment allegation, the company must investigate promptly. Then, based on the investigation, it will decide what steps to take next.

Sometimes the company will conclude that no harassment occurred. Even if that's the case, it should consider whether anything else should be done. Was there a misunderstanding to address? Will it still be too toxic to have certain employees working together?

And when there is a finding of harassment, the range of potential consequences is broad. In minor cases, it may be enough for the individuals involved to be reminded of the anti-harassment policy, made aware of the concerns, and directed not to retaliate or repeat the unwelcome behavior. Other times, the company should discipline the offender(s). This can range from a verbal or written warning up to termination of employment.

You must also consider whether to act beyond the people involved in specific instances of harassment. Is it time to conduct anti-harassment training across the organization, or at least in one department or segment of the company? Does the anti-harassment policy need to be updated?

Anti-Harassment Training

Anti-harassment training is a key component of avoiding liability in this area.

Yes, training employees involves costs. The company not only has to pay someone to conduct the training, but it also must invest the time of its employees to participate. But even though most employers are not strictly required to provide anti-harassment training, it's really too costly not to.

Still not convinced? Here are five reasons employers should provide anti-harassment training:

1. The Law Requires It (Where Applicable)

A few states require employers to provide sexual harassment training. New York does not when this book is being released. But that will likely change in 2018 based on pending legislation in response to the recent attention to sexual harassment issues. So, here's a quick look at what is already required elsewhere.

In California and Connecticut, employers with 50+ employees must provide two hours of sexual harassment prevention training to all supervisors in the state. Covered employers must provide the training within six months of hire or promotion. California also requires retraining of these employees at least every two years.

Maine requires employers with 15+ employees to conduct a sexual harassment education and training program for all new employees in their first year of employment. More in-depth training is required for management and supervisory employees.

Several other states require training for some employees, most typically those employed by the state itself.

Note: The few laws that require training are limited to *sexual harassment*. However, I think it is usually best not to limit anti-harassment training to harassment based on sex. This approach disproportionately targets women as victims and men as harassers. A discussion of various protected characteristics brings everyone into the mix as a potential victim and harasser— obviously with the goal of having no one be either!

2. It Creates a Defense to Employee Claims

Even employers who are not in states that require them to provide anti-harassment training have good law-based reasons for doing so. Under most state and federal employment discrimination laws, the courts recognize a possible defense for employers who have taken reasonable efforts to prevent harassment. This is commonly known as the *Faragher/Ellerth* defense, based on the names of two U.S. Supreme Court cases.

This defense doesn't help where the alleged harassment resulted in a "tangible employment action," which could include reduction in pay, denial of promotion, or termination, for example.

In other cases, the *Faragher/Ellerth* defense may apply if the employer can show that:

(a) The employer exercised reasonable care to prevent and promptly correct any harassing behavior; and

(b) The employee unreasonably failed to take advantage of any preventive or corrective opportunities by the employer or otherwise unreasonably failed to avoid harm.

As a practical matter, establishing this defense requires the employer to at least have an anti-harassment policy and an effective complaint procedure. Okay, so where does the training come in?

If nothing else, anti-harassment training goes a long way in helping an employer establish that employees knew about the anti-harassment policy and how to file a complaint! Ideally, the training will also encourage employees to report relatively minor incidents earlier, so they don't escalate into more serious situations. The company's prompt response in such cases can further prove the effectiveness of its policy and procedures.

3. Good Employees Will Behave Better

No one is arguing that if every employer provided anti-harassment training it would stop workplace harassment entirely. There's not even good data that it will meaningfully deter the people most likely to engage in unlawful harassment. But let's look at what it probably does do.

Think about a model employee, at least from a behavior standpoint. This may be the person most likely to change behavior following anti-harassment training. He or she hardly ever makes inappropriate comments to co-workers in the first place. But that doesn't mean they are perfect and always avoid making others uncomfortable. Good training will demonstrate subtle ways they may occasionally offend others. Well-behaved employees will readily pick up on these examples and conform their behavior. They'll become even more pleasant to work with and less likely to offend other employees.

Perhaps even more important, training can empower these good employees to recognize when others cross the line. Ideally, it will give them the knowledge and encouragement to speak up, either directly to the harasser or to human resources, etc. Or at least it will show them the value of speaking to those who suffer harassment from others to offer support.

4. Bad Employees Will Be Stopped

It would be nice to think that good training will deter employees from engaging in harassment. But the employees most likely to offend others may also be those least likely to accept readily that they're doing anything wrong.

The good news is that because your organization hopefully has many more "good employees" than "bad" ones, the training can still reduce incidents of harassment. Training can show employees how to stand up for themselves and others. This can help end harassment as soon as it starts. Or if harassment persists, the victims and their co-workers will know how to report it. Then it's just up to the organization to investigate appropriately and take the right action to correct the situation.

5. It Sends the Right Message

Admittedly, most employees don't look forward to attending anti-harassment training. But they can't deny that workplace harassment is a very serious matter. And many, especially those who have felt victimized by harassment, will appreciate their employer's efforts to address the subject.

Put differently, what does it say if a company doesn't provide anti-harassment training? At best, it suggests acceptance of harassment as inevitable and unavoidable. At worst, it appears the organization is indifferent to harassment. Providing the training doesn't cost enough to justify either message.

Discrimination Complaints

Despite good policies and training, harassment or other forms of discrimination may still occur. Or employees may at least perceive that they have. Let's look at what happens then.

Internal Employment Discrimination Complaints

Sometimes employees will make employment discrimination complaints to their employers directly. They may first complain to human resources, a supervisor, or perhaps an owner of the company. These complaints should always be taken seriously. As discussed, employers may sometimes have legal defenses based on whether they have been made aware of alleged discrimination and how they responded to the allegations. Obviously, evidence that legitimate complaints were ignored will not help the employer's case!

A lead investigator (often an HR professional) should then investigate the allegations. This will usually begin with interviewing the complaining employee. If applicable, other witnesses and the alleged discriminator(s) should also be interviewed. Once the investigator has completed the investigation, they should prepare findings and recommend an outcome. The results should usually be conveyed to the complaining employee. Additional employees, such as alleged harassers and relevant supervisors may also need to be notified.

If warranted, the employer may take disciplinary action against one or more employees. Sometimes appropriate corrective action will instead involve changing workplace policies, procedures, etc. In other cases, the aggrieved employee may receive a job change, compensation correction, or other modification to remedy the perceived discrimination.

Employment Discrimination Complaints to Governmental Agencies

Often New York employees have a choice of filing employment discrimination complaints with either the New York State Division of Human Rights or EEOC. There are also some local civil rights agencies within the state, such as the New York City Commission on Human Rights. A complaint filed with one of these agencies may be cross-filed with another. Usually, however, one agency takes the lead in investigating a complaint.

Once one of these agencies receives a complaint that is valid on its face, they send a copy of it to the employer involved. Employers are first given the opportunity to submit a position statement and relevant documents in response to the allegations made in the complaint. Companies should take this step very seriously, as it sets the basis for their defense to the claims. Most employers should involve legal counsel familiar with responding to employment discrimination claims at this stage.

The position statement will explain the company's side of the story. Sometimes the employee's account is accurate, but incomplete. Other times, it is inaccurate in the first place. Either way the employer may know more about the circumstances than the employee does.

Once the agency receives the employer's position statement, it typically sends it to the complaining employee for review and comment. Therefore, a complete, well-written position statement can be used not only to show the government investigator that no discrimination occurred, but also to demonstrate to the employee that they weren't wronged in the way they thought they were. This can sometimes persuade the employee to withdraw (or at least lose interest in) their complaint.

After receiving the position statement and any rebuttal statement from the complainant, the agency may conduct further investigation. This can include a request for additional documents or other evidence or interviews with individuals involved. When interviewing (non-complainant) supervisory employees, the agency will usually allow an attorney representing the company to be present. The investigators may seek contact information to enable them to speak to non-supervisors directly, without employer representatives present.

Sometimes the agencies will hold investigatory conferences where both the employer and complainant will be present together. These may occur either by phone or in person. Typically, the investigator asks all the questions, and the parties do not get to cross-examine each other. Nonetheless, employers should have legal representation by this stage. Attorneys can help ensure that the most helpful information is presented. Plus, it is best that the attorney observes all witnesses present for the investigative conference in case the matter proceeds to a hearing or further litigation.

Often investigators will conclude an investigatory conference by requesting additional information from either or both parties. After all information is submitted, the agency will determine whether to proceed with the case.

Possible Outcomes of Agency Investigations

After completing its investigation, the New York State Division of Human Rights will issue either a "Probable Cause" or "No Probable Cause" finding. If it finds Probable Cause, then the case will continue to a public hearing. The hearing is like a court trial but is somewhat less formal and usually held in a conference room rather than a courtroom. A No Probable Cause finding ends the administrative case in favor of the employer; however, employees can appeal the agency's determination through the courts.

In most cases the EEOC will issue a Notice of Right to Sue to the employee regardless of its investigatory findings. This Notice gives the complaining party 90 days to file a lawsuit in court under the applicable federal employment discrimination statutes. The Notice of Right to Sue will further identify the basis for the dismissal, essentially again indicating whether the EEOC found any support for the charge of discrimination. However, the EEOC's finding does not determine the outcome of a subsequent court case.

If it finds a case particularly worthy of pursuing, the EEOC can sue on its own behalf against the employer based on an employee's discrimination claim. Given limited enforcement resources, the EEOC only takes a small percentage of charges to litigation. Often these are cases affecting numerous employees or featuring especially egregious examples of discrimination.

Don't Forget This Part

It's not the end of the world if your company receives an employment discrimination complaint. With the proliferation of laws protecting employees, any organization with employees can be hit with a complaint at any time. Sometimes there is just a misunderstanding that needs to be worked out. Other times the process will take longer to resolve, but employers often prevail in these matters.

And please obtain legal advice—especially once an administrative agency like the New York State Division of

Human Rights, New York Civil Rights Commission, or the EEOC gets involved! Experienced employment lawyers can offer various levels of assistance with the process depending on your needs and circumstances.

No Retaliation

When employers receive complaints of harassment, they must ensure that no one retaliates against the person who made the complaint, the victim of harassment, or any other employees involved in bringing the complaint forward.

Investigators must remind the subjects of harassment investigations that they cannot retaliate. Any retaliation that nonetheless occurs must be taken seriously.

Retaliation includes any adverse action, not just formal job-related consequences. It can even include acts outside the workplace and things done after the employee has left employment.

EEOC Discrimination Charges in 2017

So, how common are formal complaints of employment discrimination? The EEOC publishes annual data on charges filed throughout the United States on the laws it oversees. This does not include claims filed with state or local agencies, such as the New York State Division of Human Rights or New York City Human Rights Commission. Nonetheless, it shows some interesting workplace realities and trends.

At the time of publication of this book, the most recent annual data was released in January 2018. This Fiscal Year 2017 Enforcement and Litigation Data reports that the EEOC resolved 99,109 discrimination charges in the fiscal year ending September 30, 2017. The EEOC had a remaining charge workload of 61,621, the lowest year-end level in 10 years. Among other raw statistics of note, the EEOC received over 540,000 calls and 155,000+ inquiries in its field offices across the country. It recovered nearly $400 million on behalf of victims of alleged discrimination.

Bases of EEOC Discrimination Charges

In FY 2017, retaliation was the most common grounds for EEOC discrimination charges. Nearly half of all charges included an allegation of retaliation (48.8%).

Three protected characteristics each appeared in nearly one-third of all FY 2017 EEOC discrimination charges: race (33.9%), disability (31.9%), and sex (30.4%). Age discrimination was the next most prevalent allegation, appearing in 21.8% of charges.

Five other categories protected by laws that the EEOC enforces each appeared in less than 10% of the charges:

- National Origin – 9.8%
- Religion – 4.1%
- Color – 3.8%
- Equal Pay Act – 1.2%
- Genetic Information – 0.2%

Sexual Harassment Charges

Sexual harassment is only one subset of the 25,605 sex discrimination charges that the EEOC received in FY 2017. Most cases were claims of disparate treatment (favoring one sex over the other), such as regarding employment, promotion, or compensation.

The EEOC received 6,696 charges alleging sexual harassment. It obtained $46.3 million on behalf of sexual harassment victims.

Perhaps surprising given recent media attention, the number of charges alleging sexual harassment declined in FY 2017. They have steadily gone down over the past decade. But the Harvey Weinstein report (followed by many others) did not break until the end of the last EEOC fiscal year. Thus, it will be interesting to revisit this statistic for fiscal year 2018.

Other Trends in EEOC Discrimination Charges

The EEOC received fewer charges in FY 2017 (84,254) than it had in any year since FY 2007 (82,792). Last year's total was down 7.9% from FY 2016.

The number of charges alleging discrimination based on race, sex, national origin, religion, age, and genetic information all reached the lowest levels in at least five, and in several cases 10+, years.

On the other hand, EEOC charges alleging discrimination based on color reached a 20-year high. Retaliation claims reached their highest proportion of total claims during that same period, continuing a steady upward trend. Disability claims also continued to increase as a percentage of total EEOC discrimination charges.

Geographic Origin of EEOC Cases

Employees of all states may file discrimination charges with the EEOC. In many states, like New York, employees also have the option of filing with a state agency that investigates claims under state employment discrimination laws. The varying procedures and substantive grounds for claims under respective state laws may affect the frequency of EEOC cases in a state. The EEOC's reported statistics do not include charges filed with state or local Fair Employment Practices Agencies.

In FY 2017, 10.5% of all EEOC discrimination charges were filed in Texas. Florida had the second most charges at 8.1%. California was third with 6.4% of charges. These are the also the three most populous states (though California has by far the most residents).

Despite being the fourth largest state by population, New York only accounted for the 8th most EEOC discrimination charges (4.4%). In part, this may be because many employees pursue their claims under the New York State or New York City Human Rights Laws instead of federal law.

EEOC Litigation

Though it has litigation authority, the EEOC does not go to court over many of the charges it receives. The agency filed 184 discrimination lawsuits in FY 2017. This included 124 cases alleging discrimination against an individual, 30 cases involving multiple victims or discriminatory policies, and 30 systemic discrimination cases. The EEOC reports a "successful outcome" in 90.8% of its resolved cases. The agency ended the year with 242 active court cases.

CHAPTER 6–LABOR RELATIONS

The National Labor Relations Act (NLRA) affords certain statutory rights to employees, employers, and labor organizations (usually known as "unions"). Among the NLRA's provisions are those permitting workers to organize (i.e., join a union) for collective bargaining. In addition, the Act gives individual employees the right to engage in concerted activity for their mutual aid and protection with respect to terms and conditions of employment *even if the employees are not represented by or seeking to join a union.*

The NLRA permits labor organizations to represent employees as a spokesperson for a "bargaining unit." As defined by the law, unions "exist for the purpose, in whole or in part, of dealing with employers concerning grievances, labor disputes, wages, rates of pay, hours of employment or conditions of work."

Companies can voluntarily recognize unions upon a showing of employee support. But more often they only recognize unions as their employees' representative after an election run by the National Labor Relations Board (NLRB). If the union wins the election, then the employer must bargain with the union and can no longer deal directly with employees in the covered bargaining unit over the terms and conditions of employment.

Unions secure their revenue by charging their members dues. They may also raise money by charging an initiation fee for new members, levying special assessments on members, or fining members for violating union rules.

Most states in the U.S. are now "right-to-work" states. In those states, employees may not be compelled to join the union or to pay any union dues. New York is not, however, a right-to-work state. In fact, even for the small subset of private-sector companies not subject to NLRB jurisdiction, New York law provides an alternative basis and procedures for employees to join unions and become represented in dealing with their employers under the New York State Employment Relations Act.

The NLRB has become a highly political and highly partisan agency. This has resulted in much uncertainty for employers regarding the application of the NLRA. For example, during President Barack Obama's administration, the NLRB actively promoted unionization and the expansion of employee rights in the workplace. Under President Donald Trump, the five-member Board shifted to majority-Republican control. Even within Trump's first year, this prompted significant reversals of Obama-era rulings.

Recent Policy Shifts

Republicans (temporarily) lost majority control of the NLRB when Chairman Philip Miscimarra's term expired on December 16, 2017. Facing a 2-2 party split to begin 2018, the two other Republican Members (who were appointed by President Trump) joined the outgoing Chairman in issuing pivotal rulings in the last days of his term. Here's a quick summary of some of the most impactful 2017 NLRB policy shifts.

New Election Rules?

Not yet. But the road is paved.

On December 13, 2017, the NLRB issued a Request for Information from the public regarding the agency's union election procedures. Specifically, the Board asked for information regarding the 2014 amendments to the rules. Those were promulgated by a Democrat-majority Board under President Obama, leading to what many have dubbed "quickie elections."

Under these rules, elections typically occur about 23 days after the union files an election petition, compared to 38 days under the old rules. This is about 40% faster, giving companies much less time to react to an election petition and inform employees why they don't need the union.

The Request for Information itself does not change anything. However, it does strongly suggest a potential change in course as early as 2018. The most notable result would likely be more time between filing of petitions and elections taking place.

More Reasonable Restrictions on Employee Conduct

Under the previous administration, the NLRB said that employers could not have policies requiring employees to be "respectful."

That was only illustrative of the extent to which the "Obama Board" objected to standard employment policies of the types long found in many companies' employee handbooks. (And remember, this includes companies where no union represents any employees.)

The Obama NLRB also particularly focused on regulating comparatively new "social media" policies. Various Democrat-controlled panels routinely struck down policies, or at least portions of them, that seemed to most employers to be reasonable means of conducting business and avoiding undue attacks on companies from their own employees.

On December 14, 2017, the Miscimarra-chaired Board effectively reversed numerous Obama-era decisions by changing the legal test upon which they were decided.

A 2004 NLRB decision reasoned that even if a rule doesn't "explicitly restrict" an employee right under the NLRA, the rule may still be unlawful if employees would "reasonably construe the language" to restrict activity that the Act protects.

In a case involving Boeing, the 2017 NLRB (with both Democrats dissenting) rejected that standard and replaced it with a "balancing" test. Going forward, the NLRB will now weigh "the nature and extent of the potential impact on NLRA rights" against "legitimate justifications associated with the rule."

The likely impact of the new test will be greater protection of employers' rights to maintain control over their business.

Some seemingly innocuous company rules that have long been found to violate the NLRA may still be unlawful despite this philosophy shift. For example, the NLRB has historically invalidated rules that prohibit employees from discussing their compensation with other employees. (This is now protected by other state and local laws in New York as well.)

Eliminating Micro-Units

In 2011, the NLRB issued a ruling that has permitted unions to organize smaller subsets of a company's workforce. Essentially, the Obama Board would accept most any bargaining unit containing employees who share *some* "community of interest." The employer had the burden of proving that additional employees share an "*overwhelming* community of interest" to enlarge the scope of a proposed bargaining unit.

The new line of cases beginning in 2011 benefited unions seeking to organize, because they did not need to win the support of as many employees within a workplace. Indeed, they had greater latitude to pursue bargaining units that coincided with employees who favored union representation. Pockets of co-workers who opposed the union could be ignored.

On December 15, 2017, the new Republican majority reinstated the NLRB's traditional community of interest standard in determining which bargaining units are appropriate. Under this restored test, the Board will evaluate "whether the employees in a petitioned-for group share a community of interest sufficiently distinct from the interests of employees excluded from the petitioned-for group to warrant a finding that the proposed group constitutes a separate appropriate unit."

Are Unions Bad? Tips for Employers

Most companies don't want their employees to organize a union in their workplace. Fundamentally, unions tend to increase costs and reduce management flexibility.

Here's how unions can mean more time at the table and less time getting the work done.

Unions Are Businesses Too

Like your company, a union is a business. Most unions have employees. Employees who work for unions can even form their own unions (and often do). But we're focusing on the situation where unions represent employees of a company other than a union—like a manufacturing facility or a construction company.

Unions make money by collecting dues from the company's employees. Often the employer must withhold the dues from its employees' pay and transfer the money over to the union. This is money out of the pocket of the company's employees. Beyond dues, unions can also levy initiation fees, assessments, and fines on its members. Unions use this money to pay for their employees and other business expenses.

Union business is somewhat circular. Union organizers work to get their unions into your workplace. Then your employees pay dues to the union. The union uses the dues money to pay the organizers. If you look at it this way, union organizers are salespeople who make money by selling a product: union representation.

To be sure, unions perform other services beyond unionizing. They also engage in lobbying, represent bargaining units in negotiations, and deal with day-to-day workplace disputes, including grievances and arbitrations. Employee dues pay for these functions as well. On one hand, if a union must work hard to earn this money, this means there are a lot of problems in the workplace. On the other hand, if there aren't problems, then employees may feel like they're not getting much for their money from the union.

Here's the first key lesson for employers (**Tip #1**): Keep your workers happy, and they won't need to "hire" a union. Or if they already have one, they may decide to "fire" it if they perceive that they don't need it anymore.

Unions Prevent Dealing Directly with Employees

Once a union becomes the representative of a group of employees, the employer must deal with the union directly regarding most terms and conditions of employment. This typically starts with negotiating a collective bargaining agreement. This is the contract that determines wages, benefits, discipline, and other matters affecting all employees in the represented bargaining unit.

It can take a long time—many months—to reach agreement on a contract with the union. In the meantime, employers' hands are largely tied. They can't unilaterally change wages, benefits, etc., unless the negotiations have reached an "impasse." And the union doesn't always agree there is an impasse, so an employer often acts at its own risk by making a change without union consent. This is true during the life of a labor contract as well.

If an employee wants a raise, the company can't grant it without union approval. And unions typically insist on lockstep compensation where seniority determines employees' wages. If new employees are more skilled, they will still make less money than a longer tenured employee who is not as talented.

The collective bargaining agreement may also control many aspects of scheduling, include overtime assignments. It can be difficult to work with an individual employee to do what may be best for both the employee and the company because of the strict requirements of the contract.

Tip #2: If you do have a union, it's usually best to have a good relationship with its leaders. Not every aspect of the union-employer relationship should be a fight. Good labor relations foster more flexibility from both sides and should make things run smoother.

Job Protection Isn't Always Just

Without a union, the default is that employees are employed "at will." This means they can resign or be let go for any reason with or without notice. But under union contracts, an employer usually can't discipline an employee without "just cause."

It may surprise you that no one really knows exactly what "just cause" is. Ultimately, it's whatever the arbitrator (or perhaps a court) says it is in a given case. If a company disciplines an employee and the employee doesn't like it, then the employee or the union can file a grievance. If the company doesn't change the discipline to something the employee accepts, then the case may proceed to arbitration, requiring a hearing. Then the arbitrator hears both sides' version of the situation and decides whether to uphold the discipline as imposed.

In my experience, companies don't go around trying to get rid of good employees. So, at least in cases of termination, disciplinary grievances are most often serving one of two purposes: (1) contesting the supervisor's motives or competence or (2) appeasing a bad employee. Sometimes the former has merit. But the latter seems to be more common.

The real problem is that grieving and arbitrating a bad employee's discipline costs the union time and money. The money comes from the dues of all the employees. Most of them are good employees who will never grieve discipline. This is because either they won't be disciplined, or they'll accept they deserved it. Thus, the good employees end up paying to support the bad employees.

Tip #3: Hire good employees and hope they keep the bad ones in check. I know this tip seems overly simplistic. But the point is that it really pays to invest in good hiring methods—including with respect to labor relations issues. (But, to be clear, you can't refuse to hire someone based on their past union activity to prevent them from organizing your company's employees!)

Employees Can Sue Unions

In case you're wondering why unions spend good employees' money to defend bad employees. . . . Unions owe the employees they represent a "duty of fair representation." That basically means they must represent all employees fairly. (Well, I guess that was obvious!)

There is a high standard for an employee to sue a union for breach of the duty of fair representation. The union must have been reckless in its treatment of an employee (or group of employees). But, like most everyone else, unions don't like to be sued. So, they typically err on the side of caution and try to defend everyone who wants to contest their discipline.

Tip #4: To claim that the union has breached its duty of fair representation, an employee also must allege that the employer has breached the collective bargaining agreement. Makes sense, right? The union had no duty to represent the employee if the company didn't do something wrong. As a result, in these cases the union and employer essentially end up on the same side of the table opposite the employee. This is another of many reasons why, if you have a union, you should try to maintain a professional working relationship, even if you won't always agree.

Good Employers Don't Need Unions

You're a good employer, right? If you took the time to read this far into this book, you probably are. There may be flaws in your game, but you're at least trying to do right by your employees.

Management and supervision are critical in rendering unions unnecessary. Unions can promise higher wages and better benefits, but only the employer can make those things a reality. So, the company *should* always have the upper hand. But if its supervisors demean, ignore, or otherwise mistreat employees, they'll look for someone else to protect them. That's when union organizers get a foot in the door.

If you are a good employer that already has a union in your workplace, then your goal is to improve your relationship with both the union and the employees to the point where it's not so bad that the union is around. Then maybe at some point the employees will wonder why they are paying the union to be there at all.

CHAPTER 7-ENDING EMPLOYMENT

Every employment relationship eventually comes to an end. The separation can either be voluntary or involuntary from the employee's perspective. Voluntary separations include retirements or resignations. Involuntary separations generally result either from poor performance, misconduct, or economic reduction of the workforce.

This chapter primarily focuses on involuntary terminations of employment. However, some of the information here would apply to voluntary separations as well.

We'll start with something practical and weave in more technical legal matters as we move toward the end of the chapter (and the book, but don't ignore the helpful appendices that follow).

Tips for Firing Problem Employees

Employees are critical to the success of any company. But sometimes problem employees cause more trouble than they are worth. At that point, the best decision may be to move on.

There are many things to consider when firing problem employees. Here are some tips to get you started:

1. Don't Do It on Friday

Okay, this is not the most absolute piece of advice in this book. There may be occasions when you must give an employee the bad news at the end of the week. But it usually shouldn't be your first choice.

Why? Because it just doesn't go over as well.

First, it's not ideal for whomever will inform the employee that they're out. That's usually not an easy conversation to have. On Friday it's natural for even the most dedicated managers to look forward to some downtime over the weekend. Why send them off haunted by an emotional firing on Friday afternoon?

Second, the same sentiment applies to the employee being fired. They often haven't done anything so wrong that it's worth destroying their weekend either. Consider letting them enjoy the weekend and then give them the bad news on Monday.

Third, although perhaps decreasingly true in our modern 24/7 society, the employee still has less of the world open to them on the weekend. Lawyers, doctors, accountants, counselors, etc., are all still much more likely to be unavailable before the next week starts. So, you may be sending a now disgruntled former employee off with nowhere to turn for a couple days.

Fourth, your company probably isn't fully operational on the weekend either. There may be things you need to transition, ranging from calling customers to on-boarding a replacement. Not all of these tasks are urgent, but some may be. When you let someone go earlier in the week, you can probably move on faster.

2. Have a Good Reason

Yes, many employees have "at-will" employment. That theoretically means they can be let go for any reason or no reason at all. However, as we've discussed, there are numerous employment discrimination laws that an employee may rely on to contest their discharge. Thus, the company should definitely have and identify a good reason for firing an employee before it does so.

For problem employees, this shouldn't be too hard. Good reasons for letting someone go include poor work performance, attendance problems, bad attitude, misconduct, etc. Just make sure you know the answer to the question, "why did you fire me?" before you do it.

That being said, you don't necessarily have to tell the employee every detail of the decision. Still, you should be prepared to make a general statement about your reasoning. And I mean something more than "it just isn't working out." Employees often interpret that vague assertion as a cover-up for some improper basis. They may hear "you're too old," "we're tired of accommodating your disability," or "we really want a man for this job." You should say enough to make it clear none of those is what you mean. Otherwise, you might find yourself responding to a discrimination complaint.

3. Don't Leave Room for Debate

When the decision has been made to move on from an employee, it's time to tell them and move on. Some employees will refuse to accept the words "we're letting you go." They'll try to debate management's assessment of their performance, make excuses for their attendance issues, promise to do better, etc. It's too late for any of that at this point.

You may find yourself using the exact words, "the decision is final." That's fine. Accept that most employees won't like the decision. They will be emotional in some way. This is not the time to have a back-and-forth conversation. Tell them what they need to know—"don't come back tomorrow," "we'll pack up your stuff and deliver it to your home," "here's your final paycheck"—and send them on their way.

You aren't being heartless here. You're trying to end a difficult situation as smoothly as possible. You can and should let them know whom to contact if they have questions. But give them some time to process the news before they ask those questions: "Call tomorrow." "Call next week."

4. Cut Off Their Access

Most people, even problem employees, are generally trustworthy. They're probably not going to try to nefariously sabotage your business just because they've been fired. But that doesn't mean you shouldn't take precautions.

In the termination meeting, you will obviously ask for keys, ID cards, access badges, etc. If possible, you want those immediately. If they're back at the employee's desk or at home, then you must address that. Have a checklist. Get everything back as soon as possible. If necessary under the circumstances, you may even decide to change locks.

These days many employees also have electronic access to various company systems: logins, passwords, email, etc. The best practice in most situations is to have someone cut off the employee's access while someone else tells them they are being let go. That way the employee can't leave the meeting and still get into company email or documents from his smartphone or laptop from his car, home, etc.

5. Preserve Their Computer

If the employee had a portable company computer, you'll obviously be wanting that back immediately. Ideally, that would be before they walk out the building. But if it's at home, then the employee may be able to access it before returning it. Either way, you should consider whether there could be something on the computer that should be preserved exactly as it was upon return to the company.

You should ask the same question for an employee's desktop computer in the office. Could it ever be relevant what they did on the computer? Might it support the reasons for their termination? Have they been copying company information to use against you? Or even just are there documents that they have been working on that you will need in order to pick up where they left off?

If there is any reasonable chance the employee's computer contents could be critical in some way going forward, you might want to have the hard drive forensically imaged (i.e., perfectly copied). This will preserve the computer exactly as the employee left it. Then you can still use the equipment and the data on it as necessary for the business. But if anything comes up later, you can use the backup copy to prove what the employee was doing.

6. Move on from Problem Employees

If there are lessons to learn from the situation that didn't work out, then learn them. Should you restructure the position? Was the hiring process defective? Do you need to provide more training up front? Could the supervisor(s) be more effective?

At the same time, it could just be the person who didn't work out. Don't project their failings on the next person in the job.

Also, don't reduce your standards. Just because the new person is better than the last person (who clearly wasn't good enough), that doesn't mean that the new person is meeting your standards. The next person might not work out either.

Once you have had to fire one person in a position, use the experience to know what to look for in the next employee. Start monitoring those things earlier, provide additional training and supervision where warranted, document deficiencies, and make the difficult decision sooner if necessary. Eventually you will find the right employee.

Can I Fire an Employee Over the Phone?

You've decided that an employee must go. But now you need to figure out how to do it. For most people, firing someone isn't fun. And the thought of doing it face-to-face is daunting. So, you arrive at the question, can I fire an employee over the phone?

Well, the short answer is "Yes." You *can* fire an employee over the phone, or by letter, or email. I suppose you could even send a text these days.

However, the longer answer is, you probably *shouldn't* fire an employee over the phone, unless there are compelling circumstances.

Why You Usually Shouldn't Fire an Employee Over the Phone

In the last section, I provided some advice on how to let a problem employee go. It includes important considerations such as cutting off access to company data and preserving their computer. It also suggests that you be direct and not debate the decision to end their employment. If necessary, you can follow all the same advice when firing an employee remotely. But there are many advantages to doing it in person.

Here are just several reasons you may not want to fire an employee over the phone:

1. It's less personal and may offend the employee. As a result, they may become more problematic as a former employee than they would have otherwise.

2. You can't get company property back immediately. They may still have keys, credit cards, computers, etc. You will have to arrange to recover that later and may not be able to control what the now potentially disgruntled former employee does with them in the meantime.

3. They can't take personal belongings with them as they leave. So, you will have to arrange to clean out their desk, etc., where it may have been easier to let the person do it before they left.

4. It's harder to evaluate how the person takes the news. Sometimes it is important to read whether the employee was surprised or not. Or whether they are unduly upset, such that they may cause further disruption for the business.

5. Bad connections can interfere with the message. Telephone calls break in and out. Plus, you don't have the eye contact or view of body language that is important in serious conversations. Video calls don't necessarily solve these problems and may lead to even more technological interruption.

6. In some cases there may be a contract, policy, or practice that establishes the procedure for notifying an employee

of their termination. For example, a collective bargaining agreement may require that a union representative be present.

7. You can't provide and go over necessary paperwork as easily. This may include written exit interviews, severance packages, or insurance information.

When You Might Need to Fire an Employee Over the Phone

We don't live in a perfect world. Even if all the above reasons not to fire an employee over the phone apply in your situation, you might have to do it anyway.

Here are several situations when you might need to fire an employee over the phone:

1. The employee isn't available to meet in person. They could be hospitalized, traveling, or even in jail. These all happen, and sometimes you can't wait until a physical meeting is possible before sharing the news.

2. There is legitimate concern that this person may become violent. There are bad people out there, and it's possible that one worked for you. If you have real fear of personal safety or that the employee will cause damage, etc., then a phone call (or letter) may be best.

3. You are firing the employee for no-call, no-show, and they still haven't shown up. Then you may be lucky to even reach them by phone. Sometimes you will have to settle for just officially notifying the employee by mail.

4. The employee refuses to meet in person. In that case, they probably already know what's coming. If possible, it

may still be better to try to find someone they will meet with before resorting to a phone call.

5.   There isn't time to meet in person. This should be a rare situation where the employee is remote, such as traveling for business, but must be stopped immediately from acting on the company's behalf.

Employee Releases

Sometimes you want to do more than just send an employee out the door. Either by policy or because of the specific situation, the company may want to pursue a formal severance with the employee. This can include providing payment or other benefits to the employee in exchange for the employee's release of potential claims against the company.

Unless you have significant experience with this situation, you probably will want to involve an attorney in this process. But, if you do have an experienced employment attorney assisting, here's something you can expect to hear about.

The Older Workers Benefit Protection Act (OWBPA) was a 1990 amendment to the federal Age Discrimination in Employment Act of 1967 (ADEA), which prohibits discrimination against employees 40 years or older because of their age. This is relevant here, because the OWBPA includes specific requirements that employers must meet if they want to obtain enforceable employee releases of ADEA claims. Age discrimination claims are often not the only, or even primary, claims the company wants the employee to release as part of a severance package. But, the OWBPA still merits consideration in most cases where employee releases are sought.

Yes, formally the OWBPA only applies to waiver of ADEA claims. Accordingly, many employers choose not to follow all of its requirements for releases by employees under the age of 40. However, an employee could challenge any waiver as unenforceable on basic legal principles. Essentially, employees could claim they did not understand what they were signing. Using the OWBPA requirements for all employment releases promotes greater enforceability. If it is good enough for Congress and its federal age discrimination law, shouldn't it be good enough for all employee waivers?

To reiterate, many employee releases should still be enforceable even if they don't satisfy all aspects of the OWBPA. But it's usually not worth taking that risk.

OWBPA Requirements for Employee Releases

1. The waiver of claims must be part of a written agreement between the employee and the employer. The agreement must be written in a manner "calculated to be understood by such individual, or the average individual eligible to participate."

2. The release must specifically refer to rights or claims arising under the ADEA.

3. The employee cannot waive rights or claims that may arise after the release is signed.

4. The employee must receive something of value in exchange for the waiver of rights. It must be something that the employee did not already have the right to receive.

5. The employer must advise the employee in writing to consult with an attorney before signing the release agreement.

6. The employer must give the employee at least 21 days to consider the release agreement.

7. The release agreement must give the employee at least seven days after signing to revoke the agreement. The agreement does not become enforceable before the end of the revocation period.

Additional Requirements for Group Programs

The OWBPA contains additional requirements for waivers connected to an "exit incentive or other employment termination programs offered to a group or class of employees." This includes both voluntary and involuntary programs. Thus, it applies both to voluntary resignation programs and involuntary reductions in force. Most likely, it applies to any situation where the company asks more than one employee to sign a release related to the same decisionmaking process. It does not necessarily apply, however, when an employer fires two employees around the same time, but for unrelated reasons.

For group programs, the employer must allow employees least 45 days to consider the release agreement, rather than 21. In addition, the employer must give the following information to employees at the beginning of the 45-day consideration period:

• A description of any class, unit or group of employees covered by the program, any eligibility factors, and any applicable time limits; and

• A list of job titles and ages of all employees eligible or selected for the program, and the ages of all employees in the same job classification or organizational unit who are not eligible or selected for the program.

Many employers especially hesitate to provide the age lists required in group programs. However, failing to do so would render the waiver of ADEA claims unenforceable.

Worker Adjustment and Retraining Notification

Here's another relatively intricate legal framework related to some terminations—specifically, group terminations.

State and federal Worker Adjustment and Retraining Notification (WARN) Acts require companies to provide notice before taking certain actions to reduce the size of their workforce. For employers conducting reductions in force in New York, the state law will almost always be more restrictive. Thus, complying with New York's WARN Act will likely also satisfy the federal requirements. Nonetheless, I will note distinctions between the two laws here in discussing when the notices are required. And, as usual, there are exceptions.

Covered Employers

The federal WARN Act requires employers with at least 100 total employees to give written notice in advance of certain workforce reductions affecting at least 50 employees. New York's WARN Act applies to companies with as few as 50 total employees who take certain actions affecting as few as 25 employees.

"Part-time employees" and properly classified independent contractors do not count in determining whether a WARN event will occur. However, the definition of "part-time employee" is multifaced and likely to differ from how the company normally classifies its workers.

Timing of Notice

The federal WARN Act requires 60 days' advance written notice in the event of a "plant closing" or "mass layoff." New York's WARN Act requires 90 days' notice for these events and certain plant "relocations."

Notice Events

A "plant closing" occurs where an employment site (or one or more facilities or operating units within an employment site) will be shut down, and the shutdown will result in an "employment loss" for 25 or more employees (50 under federal law) during any 30-day period.*

A "mass layoff" occurs where there is to be a group reduction in force that does not result from a plant closing, but will result in an employment loss at the employment site during any 30-day period* for: (a) 250 or more employees (500 under federal law), or (b) 25-249 employees (for 50-499 under federal law) if they make up at least 33% of the employer's active workforce.

*Sometimes the 30-day periods referenced above extend to 90-days in determining whether WARN notices are required.

New York's WARN Act also refers to a "relocation" situation that is not part of the federal law. In New York, a "relocation" occurs where all or substantially all of the industrial or commercial operations of an employer will be removed to a different location 50 miles or more away from the original site of operation and 25 or more employees suffer an employment loss.

As used in the WARN Acts, an "employment loss" occurs in any of these situations: (a) employment terminations other than a discharge for cause, voluntary departure, or retirement; (b) layoffs exceeding six months; and (c) a reduction in an employee's hours of work of more than 50% in each month of any six-month period. Hence, companies may need to issue WARN notices even if the intention is not to permanently end the employees' employment.

Exceptions

WARN notices may not be required every time the above conditions exist. The exceptions, however, tend to be narrowly applied. Any company seeking to rely on one should discuss the matter with an attorney experienced in working with the WARN Acts.

For example, the WARN Acts recognize a "faltering company" exception. But the mere fact that the company must reduce its workforce isn't enough to qualify the exception (or else there would be no point to the laws in the first place!). This exception only applies to plant closings and is limited to situations where a company has sought new capital or business in attempt to stay open *and* giving notice would ruin the opportunity to get the new capital or business.

Similarly, an "unforeseeable business circumstances" exception applies to closings and layoffs caused by business circumstances that were not reasonably foreseeable when notice would otherwise have been required. But, the employer still must give as much notice as possible.

Some other scenarios where WARN notices may not be required, or a shorter notice period may suffice, include where:

- The company offers to transfer employees to a different work location within a reasonable commuting distance.

- The reduction of force results from the completion of a project for which the employees were hired with the understanding that their employment was only for the limited duration of the project. This might include some forms of seasonal employment.

- A new company will continue employment in connection with the sale of a business.

- A closing or layoff is the direct result of a natural disaster, such as a flood, earthquake, drought, or storm.

- The company permanently replaces economic strikers in accordance with the National Labor Relations Act.

Notice Recipients

When notices are required, they must be sent to employees, their unions (if applicable), and certain government officials.

Penalties

If a company should have given notice under WARN and does not, then it may be held liable for damages to each employee who should have received notice for up to 60 days' pay and benefits, plus civil penalties and attorneys' fees.

Unemployment

These final topics are about what happens after employees leave employment and what you might be able to do to have them stay despite financial concerns.

All New York employers must pay into the state's unemployment insurance program. When employees leave employment for non-disqualifying reasons, they may be eligible to obtain unemployment benefits. The amount of unemployment insurance benefits obtained by a company's former employees affects how much the company pays for unemployment insurance. As a result, when an individual files for unemployment, the State asks their former employer for information about the person's compensation and reason for separation from employment. This gives employers a chance to contest the applications of any former employees they feel should not receive unemployment benefits (and, thus, hopefully avoid the impact on the company's unemployment insurance costs).

To qualify for unemployment, claimants must:

- have lost employment through no fault of their own;

- have enough prior earnings from employment to establish a claim;

- be ready, willing, and able to work; and

- be actively seeking work and keeping a record of the work search.

The first element is the one that former employers are most likely to challenge. Employees who voluntarily resign from employment through no fault of the company should not receive unemployment benefits. Beyond that, the burden is typically on the employer to show it was the employee's fault they lost the job. This is not always as easy as claiming a good reason for letting them go. Typically, the unemployment insurance judges will require that the employee had express warning that specific misconduct would result in the termination of their employment. Unemployment may be denied without such notice only for the most extreme forms of misconduct (e.g., material theft, assault, and other criminal or quasi-criminal conduct). Former employees (who satisfy the earnings and job seeking requirements) will almost always receive unemployment when they have been let go only for economic, performance, or other business reasons beyond their control.

Shared Work Program

Many businesses experience ups and downs. Sometimes this results from seasonal fluctuations. Other times from unexpected conditions. Either way, a downturn in customer demand can leave employers without enough work for their existing workforce. One option employers have is to lay off employees altogether until times improve. Another option is to reduce work hours during slow periods. New York's Shared Work Program promotes the latter approach, potentially benefiting both employers and employees.

What Is the Shared Work Program?

This is special aspect of the state's unemployment insurance program that might benefit some employers and their employees.

The New York Department of Labor administers the Shared Work Program though its Unemployment Insurance Division. Through the program, employees work a reduced schedule and receive partial unemployment benefits for the same week.

Employers must apply with the Unemployment Insurance Division to participate.

Employer Eligibility

To be eligible to apply to participate in the Shared Work Program employers must have:

- At least two employees working in New York; and

- Paid Unemployment Insurance contributions, or elected reimbursement of benefits paid to former employee, for four consecutive calendar quarters.

Components of Shared Work Plans

An employer may design a Shared Work Plan to cover its total work force, specific shift(s), or work unit(s).

A proposed Shared Work Plan must:

- Reduce work hours and corresponding wages 20–60%;

- Apply only to employees who normally work no more than 40 hours per week;

- Not reduce or eliminate fringe benefits (unless also doing so for the entire work force);

- Cover a period of up to 53 weeks; and

- Replace a layoff of an equal percentage of employees

If the plan affects workers subject to a collective bargaining agreement, the employees' union(s) must also agree to participate in the Shared Work Plan.

Despite the 53-week limit on a Shared Work Plan, employers can request a new plan to begin when the current one ends.

The company cannot hire additional employees for the work group covered by the Shared Work Plan. But it can replace separated employees within the covered group.

A company with an approved plan does not have to use it each week. For weeks when employees work a full schedule, no Shared Work benefits will be paid. Employers can also change the percentage of reduction in work hours from week to week within the 20–60% range.

Employee Shared Work Program Benefits

Usually, employees can only obtain unemployment insurance benefits for weeks where they are totally unemployed. Under an approved Shared Work Plan, however, employees may apply for and receive unemployment insurance benefits even though they worked part of the week.

Although employees must be available for work for the Shared Work employer during periods of partial unemployment, they do not have to look for other work.

Employees are eligible for Shared Work benefits if they otherwise qualify for New York unemployment benefits. They may receive up to 26 weeks of regular Shared Work benefits during a benefit year.

Shared Work vs. Layoff

The Shared Work Program will not be right for all employers. However, it offers certain advantages over layoffs in some situations, including:

- Retaining valuable employees for when business picks up.

- Keeping employees engaged with the company and reducing skill deterioration.

- Lessening the impact on the company's unemployment experience rating compared to total unemployment.

- Avoiding severance pay obligations, where applicable.

Organizations who participate in the Shared Work Program still must consider related practical and legal ramifications. In some ways, reducing employee work hours can still have layoff-like consequences. It could affect rights under insurance policies, severance policies, other employee benefit plans, employment contracts, and collective bargaining agreements. In addition, it could still trigger a notice obligation under the WARN Acts.

More information about New York's Shared Work Program can be found on the NYS DOL's website (labor.ny.gov/ui/employerinfo/shared-work-program.shtm).

A NEW BEGINNING

This is where many books would have something like a "Conclusion" or "Afterward." But this is not the end of anything. Having read this book, you are now better equipped to help your organization comply with employment laws. And, probably more importantly, you should be able to add new value to your company through both your actions and inactions going forward.

Whether you're a business owner, manager, or other employee, you should focus on improving the workplace every day. There is much more to that than legal compliance. And hopefully you've learned more from this book than just what the laws say.

Don't stop here. Read on through the appendices and refer to them and the rest of the book as issues arise at work.

APPENDIX A

Top Government Websites for New York Employers

Here's a handy list of government websites that will help employers deal with employee issues:

1. U.S. Department of Labor (www.dol.gov)

The federal Department of Labor contains many relevant agencies, including:

- Bureau of Labor Statistics (BLS) (www.bls.gov)

- Occupational Safety & Health Administration (OSHA) (www.osha.gov)

- Office of Federal Contract Compliance Programs (OFCCP) (www.dol.gov/ofccp)

- Office of Labor-Management Standards (OLMS) (www.dol.gov/olms)

- Wage and Hour Division (WHD) (www.dol.gov/whd)

2. U.S. Equal Opportunity Commission (eeoc.gov)

The EEOC enforces most of the federal employment discrimination laws.

3. National Labor Relations Board (nlrb.gov)

The NLRB enforces the National Labor Relations Act. This law applies to most private-sector employers, whether they have a unionized workforce or not.

4. Internal Revenue Service (www.irs.gov)

Make sure you're withholding payroll taxes properly!

5. New York State Department of Labor (www.labor.ny.gov)

Like the federal Department of Labor, the New York State Department of Labor has many important divisions, including:

- Employment and Workforce Solutions (labor.ny.gov/dews-index.shtm)
- Labor Standards (labor.ny.gov/workerprotection/laborstandards/labor_standards.shtm)
- Unemployment Insurance (labor.ny.gov/ui/employer.shtm)

6. New York State Division of Human Rights (dhr.ny.gov)

This agency enforces the New York State Human Rights Law. Among other things, that law prohibits discrimination in employment based on numerous protected categories.

7. New York State Workers Compensation Board (www.wcb.ny.gov)

The State agency that oversees both workers comp. and disability insurance matters. It also regulates the New York Paid Family Leave Program.

8. New York State Department of Taxation and Finance (www.tax.ny.gov)

Don't forget state tax withholdings.

9. New York State Public Employment Relations Board (www.perb.ny.gov)

Despite its name, this agency now also has jurisdiction over some private employers.

Checking out these government websites won't answer all your questions, but they may point you in the right direction.

APPENDIX B

U.S. Employment Law by the Numbers

There are probably many lawyers who went to law school because they don't like dealing with numbers. I'm not one of them. So, I thought I would address some of the most significant numbers in employment law.

Many of these numbers establish thresholds, especially for coverage issues. But others are caps, dates, or other parameters.

1–Employee threshold for many employment laws

One is the number of employees an employer must have before being covered by the federal minimum wage and overtime laws. It also establishes coverage for many other federal laws, including immigration, health and safety, and labor law requirements. So, if you have just one employee, you're already responsible for employment law compliance.

$7.25–Minimum wage

This is the current nationwide minimum wage for most employees under the Fair Labor Standards Act (FLSA). Many states and some cities have higher minimum wage requirements for their employers.

11–OSHA recordkeeping threshold

Non-governmental employers with at least 11 employees must maintain records of serious work-related injuries and illnesses.

12–Annual FMLA leave allowance, in weeks

The employer can determine what 12-month period counts as a year for its employees. The best option is usually a rolling year measured back from the date on which a particular employee will use the leave. Other options include the calendar year, the employer's fiscal year, or a forward rolling year from the date the employee first takes FMLA leave.

15–Several federal discrimination laws kick in

Employers with 15+ employees are subject to Title VII of the Civil Rights Act of 1964, the Americans with Disabilities Act (ADA), and the Genetic Information Nondiscrimination Act (GINA). Title VII prohibits discrimination because of race, color, sex, religion, and national origin. The ADA prohibits discrimination against qualified individuals with disabilities and requires employers to make reasonable accommodations. GINA prohibits discrimination based on genetic information, which is broadly defined.

20–ADEA and COBRA coverage

The Age Discrimination in Employment Act (ADEA) prohibits discrimination because of age for employee 40 years of age or older.

Employers with at least 20 employees also become subject to federal COBRA insurance continuation requirements. COBRA entitles employees and/or their families to continue their group health insurance coverage for up to 18-36 months (depending on circumstances) after employment ends. The employees usually pay the coverage.

40–FLSA overtime/ADEA age thresholds

Under the FLSA, employers must pay non-exempt employees overtime once they work more than 40 hours in a work week. The overtime rate must be at least time-and-a-half the employee's regular rate.

Employees also become protected by the ADEA when they turn 40.

50–ACA, FMLA, and WARN coverages

Employers with 50+ "full-time equivalents" qualify as large employers under the Affordable Care Act (ACA). This triggers various requirements, including the obligation to provide affordable health insurance to employees (or pay a penalty).

The Family and Medical Leave Act (FMLA) applies to employers with at least 50 employees.

The federal Workforce Adjustment Retraining Notification Act (WARN) requires employers to give written notice before mass layoffs and plant closings that will cause employment loss for at least 50 employees, sometimes more.

60–Days in advance federal WARN notices must be issued

The employer must notify not only the affected employees (or their unions), but also certain government officials. There are exceptions to the notice obligation. If circumstances require the employer to act suddenly, the employer usually must give as much notice as possible.

75–FMLA geographic proximity requirement

To become eligible for FMLA leave, among other conditions, an employee must work within a 75-mile radius of at least 49 other employees.

100–WARN and EEO-1 thresholds

Non-governmental employers with 100 or more employees are potentially subject to federal WARN notice obligations and also must file annual EEO-1 reports. (Many federal contractors must file EEO-1 reports even if they have less than 100, but more than 50 employees.)

The EEO-1 form reports on company employment data by race/ethnicity, gender, and job category.

$455–Required weekly salary for some FLSA exemptions

To qualify for the most common FLSA exemptions, employees must receive a salary of at least $455 per week. The U.S. Department of Labor tried to increase this to $913 per week in 2016. Courts rejected that change, as has the current administration in Washington, which is reviewing an alternative approach.

1250–Required annual hours worked for FMLA eligibility

If an employee has not worked 1250 hours for the employer in the past 12-months, they are not eligible to take FMLA leave.

$100,000–"Highly compensated employee" exemption

The FLSA has special exemption rules for employees who receive at least $455/week in salary and $100,000/year in total compensation. These employees may be exempt even if they don't satisfy the full standard exemption tests.

$300,000–Highest cap on Title VII damages

Employers with more than 500 employees may be liable for up to $300,000 in compensatory and punitive damages for violations of Title VII's anti-discrimination provisions. The caps are lower for employers with fewer employees: 15–100 employees = $50,000; 101–200 employees = $100,000; 201–500 = $200,000.

Some state employment discrimination laws have no caps. Thus, employees often sue under both state and federal laws to maximize their potential recovery.

No caps apply to damages for lost wages/benefits or attorneys' fees under Title VII.

APPENDIX C

New York Employment Law by the Numbers

Here are some of the numbers that stand out specifically for **New York** employment law compliance.

1–Employee threshold for many employment laws

As with federal laws, many aspects of New York employment law apply to employers with as few as one employee. This includes state minimum wage/overtime, wage payment, worker's compensation, disability benefits, paid family leave, and sexual harassment laws.

4–New York Human Rights Law prohibits discrimination

New York employees of employers with at least four employees are protected by New York's employment discrimination laws. This is a much lower coverage threshold than similar federal laws. They typically don't apply until an employer has at least 15 or more employees. The New York State Human Rights Law prohibits discrimination on the basis of age, sex, sexual orientation, religion, race, national origin, disability, and predisposing genetic characteristics. It also protects employees from discrimination based on familial status, marital status, military status, and domestic violence victim status.

Note: The New York State Human Rights Law prohibits all employers, with a few as one employee, from engaging in sexual harassment.

6–Statute of limitations for wage claims, in years

New York employees can file claims for unpaid or underpaid wages going back as far as six years. This is much longer than the two- (sometimes three-) year statute of limitations under the federal Fair Labor Standards Act.

8*–Annual New York Paid Family Leave allowance, in weeks

In 2018, eligible employees may take up to 8 weeks of leave under the New York Paid Family Leave Program. In 2019, the maximum leave period increases to 10 weeks. It increases again in 2021, to 12 weeks.

$10.40–Minimum wage for Upstate employees

New York's minimum wage requirements depend on geographic location and employer size. On December 31, 2017, the base minimum wage for employees outside of New York City and Nassau, Suffolk, and Westchester counties increased to $10.40 per hour.

$11.00–Minimum wage for Long Island & Westchester employees

On December 31, 2017, the base minimum wage for employees working in Nassau, Suffolk, and Westchester counties increased to $11.00 per hour.

$12.00–Minimum wage for small New York City employers

On December 31, 2017, the base minimum wage for employees working in New York City for employers with 10 or fewer employees increased to $12.00 per hour.

$13.00–Minimum wage for large New York City employers

On December 31, 2017, the base minimum wage for employees working in New York City for employers with more than 10 employees increased to $13.00 per hour.

18–Age at which New York Human Rights Law begins to prohibit age discrimination

Unlike the federal Age Discrimination in Employment Act (ADEA), New York's employment discrimination law prohibits age discrimination against employees in both directions. The ADEA only protects employees 40 years old or older from suffering adverse employment actions because they are too old. However, the New York State Human Rights Law allows employees 18 or older to claim discrimination either because they are too old or too young.

20–Weekly hours parameter for New York Paid Family Leave

An employee's eligibility for New York Paid Family Leave depends on how many hours they are regularly scheduled to work in a week. Employees regularly scheduled to work at least 20 hours per week become eligible once they have worked for their employer for 26 consecutive weeks. Employees regularly scheduled to work less than 20 hours per week become eligible once they have worked on 175 days for the employer.

25–New York WARN notice triggering events

The New York State Workforce Adjustment Retraining Notification Act (WARN) requires employers to give written notice before mass layoffs, plant closings, and relocations that will cause employment loss for at least 25 employees, sometimes more.

30–Minimum length of meal period for most employees, in minutes

New York labor law requires that all employees who work at least six hours in a shift (sometimes less) be off duty for a meal period of at least 30 minutes. Additional time may be required in some cases.

50–New York WARN covered employer

Non-governmental employers with 50 or more employees within New York are potentially subject to New York WARN notice obligations.

90–Days in advance New York WARN notices must be issued

This is longer than the federal WARN Act's 60-day notice period. The employer must notify affected employees (and their unions, if applicable) and certain government officials. There are exceptions to the notice obligation. If circumstances require the employer to act suddenly, the employer usually must give as much notice as possible.

$780–Required salary for some New York overtime exemptions (Upstate)

New York's administrative and professional exemptions from the state's minimum wage and overtime rules require that employees receive a minimum weekly salary. As with the minimum wage, the salary requirement depends on location within the state and size of the employer. On December 31, 2017, the minimum salary for these exemptions (outside of NYC, Nassau, Suffolk, and Westchester) increased to $780 per week.

$825–Required salary for overtime exemptions (Long Island & Westchester)

On December 31, 2017, the minimum salary for these exemptions for employees in Nassau, Suffolk, and Westchester counties increased to $825 per week.

$900–Required salary for overtime exemptions (small New York City employers)

On December 31, 2017, the minimum salary for these exemptions for employees working in New York City for employers with 10 or fewer employee increased to $825 per week.

$975–Required salary for overtime exemptions (large New York City employers)

On December 31, 2017, the minimum salary for these exemptions for employees working in New York City for employers with more than 10 employees increased to $825 per week.

APPENDIX D

Employment Law Dictionary

A

ADA: The federal Americans with Disabilities Act. This law prohibits employers with 15 or more employees from discriminating against employees based on disability.

ADEA: The federal Age Discrimination in Employment Act. This law prohibits employers with 20 or more employees from discriminating against employees 40 years old or older based on age.

Administrative exemption: An exemption from minimum wage and overtime requirements for certain employees paid a sufficient salary whose primary duty is the performance of office or non-manual work directly related to the management or general business operations of the employer or the employer's customers. The employee must exercise discretion and independent judgment with respect to matters of significance.

Affirmative action: A requirement that an employer take proactive steps to improve the diversity of its workforce. This typically only applies to companies with government grants or contracts.

ALJ: An Administrative Law Judge. Many different state and federal administrative agencies use these judges to preside over hearings.

Arbitration: An alternative dispute resolution process where a neutral arbitrator decides the outcome. This is the common final step in grievance procedures between employers and unions. Individual employees can also agree to substitute arbitration for court litigation.

Arbitrator: The decision-maker in arbitrations. The parties usually mutually select the arbitrator(s) to avoid bias and partiality.

At-will: Most employees have at-will employment. This means that both they and their employer can terminate the employment at any time, for any reason, with or without notice. (But this doesn't really mean employers can fire employees for any reason, given statutory employment discrimination protections.)

B

Back pay: A common remedy for violations of employment law. Employees who prove illegal termination often recover lost wages and benefits going back to the date of termination.

Ban-the-box: Laws that prohibit employers from asking job applicants whether they have been convicted of a crime early in the hiring process.

Bargaining unit: The group of employees represented by a union for the purpose of negotiating terms and conditions of employment with their employer. Some employers have multiple bargaining units in the same facility.

C

CBA: A collective bargaining agreement. This is a common term for the contract between an employer and union regarding the terms and conditions of employment.

COBRA: The Consolidated Omnibus Budget Reconciliation Act of 1985. The name doesn't really help here. . . . This is the federal law that permits employees to continue health insurance (at their own cost) for a period of time after leaving a job. It applies to employers with 20 or more employees. However, some states, including New York, have similar laws that cover smaller employers.

Concerted activity: When employees work together regarding terms and conditions of employment. In most industries, the National Labor Relations Act protects non-supervisory employees' right to engage in concerted activity for their mutual aid and protection.

Constructive discharge: The term for what happens when an employer permits working conditions so intolerable that an employee has no choice but to quit. This usually involves ongoing or extreme harassment that violates employment discrimination laws.

Continuing violation: When harassment or discrimination occurs over time rather than as isolated incidents. A continuing violation can extend the time that an employee has to make a legal complaint of discrimination.

D

Decertification: When a group of employees chooses to no longer be represented by a union. Usually occurs through a secret ballot election after employees file a petition with the NLRB.

Disability: A protected category under state and federal employment discrimination laws. The ADA requires that an individual be substantially limited in one or more major life activities. The New York State Human Rights Law, however, essentially only requires a physical, mental, or medical impairment.

Discipline: Action taken against an employee for poor performance or misconduct. Can range from a verbal counseling to termination of employment.

Discrimination: Adverse employment action against one or more employees (or applicants) based on a protected characteristic.

Disparate impact: Discrimination that results from facially neutral policies or practices based on disproportionate negative effect on one or more groups based on a legally protected characteristic. Sometimes called unintentional discrimination.

Disparate treatment: Discrimination where an employee is treated differently based on a protected characteristic. Usually considered to be intentional discrimination.

DOL: Department of Labor. Could refer to either the United States Department of Labor or a state department, such as the New York State Department of Labor. Both the U.S. DOL and NYS DOL have broad jurisdiction with various sub-agencies regulating various aspects of the employment relationship.

Due process: Requirement that the employer act fairly in disciplining an employee, for example. Generally, a constitutional protection that only directly applies to public (government) employers. However, where employees have just cause protection, some form of due process is inherently required.

Duty of fair representation: A union's obligation to represent all members of a bargaining unit fairly and equally. Breach of this duty can serve as the basis for a lawsuit by an employee against the union, with a corresponding claim of breach of the collective bargaining agreement against the employer.

E

EAP: Employee Assistance Program. Many employers have arrangements in place to provide free and confidential assessments, short-term counseling, referrals, and follow-up services to employees who have personal and/or work-related problems.

EEOC: The U.S. Equal Employment Opportunity Commission. The agency that enforces most federal employment discrimination laws, including Title VII, the ADA, the ADEA, GINA, and the Equal Pay Act.

Employee: Someone who performs work for an employer who doesn't qualify as an independent contract (or, in limited situations, as a volunteer). Misclassifying an employee as an independent contractor causes a host of problems.

Employer: Any person or entity that permits individuals to perform work on their behalf, unless all such work is performed by bona fide independent contractors or volunteers.

Equal Pay Act: A federal law that prohibits sex discrimination in compensation for employees who perform the same work at the same location.

ERISA: The federal Employee Retirement Income Security Act. This law sets minimum standards for most voluntarily established pension and health plans in private industry. Its focus is to protect employees participating in these plans.

ESOP: Employee Stock Ownership Plan. An employee benefit plan that allows employees to purchase stock in the company with particular tax benefits.

Executive exemption: An exemption from minimum wage and overtime requirements for certain employees paid a sufficient salary whose primary duty is managing the enterprise or managing a customarily recognized department or subdivision of the enterprise. The employee must customarily and regularly direct the work of at least two other full-time employees or their equivalent.

Exempt: Most often used to refer to an employee who is not eligible to receive overtime pay. Federal and state laws have specific tests for determining which employees are exempt.

F

FLSA: The Fair Labor Standards Act. This federal law establishes minimum wage, overtime, child labor, and recordkeeping standards for most employers and employees.

FMLA: The Family and Medical Leave Act. This federal law requires employers with 50+ employees to permit qualifying employees to take unpaid leave for certain personal and family medical issues, birth/adoption/foster placement of a new child, and "qualifying exigencies" related to family member military service.

Front pay: A remedy often available when an employee prevails in a discrimination claim against an employer. These damages account for money the employee would have earned in the future had the discrimination not occurred.

G

Garnishment: The process of withholding a portion of an employee's wages to satisfy a court order, such as for child support. The employer pays the money over to the employee's third-party creditor.

Genetic information: For purposes of GINA (see below), this includes information about an individual's genetic tests and an individual's family medical history.

GINA: The Genetic Information Nondiscrimination Act. A federal law that broadly prohibits employers with 15+ employees from acquiring or using genetic information about their employees.

Grievance: A complaint, usually made by an employee or union, about terms and conditions of employment.

Grievance procedure: The process for handling workplace complaints. For unionized employees, the collective bargaining agreement commonly establishes a grievance procedure that ends in arbitration.

H

Harassment: Unlawful harassment is any conduct that is unwelcome and related to a protected status (e.g., sex or race) that is both subjectively and objectively offensive and is severe or pervasive enough to alter the terms and conditions of employment.

Hostile work environment: The broader form of unlawful harassment. Distinguishable from "quid pro quo" sexual harassment, which involves a supervisor seeking sexual conduct from an employee. Can include inappropriate conduct based on any legally protected characteristic.

Hourly: Describes an employee who earns a set amount for each hour worked. Usually, hourly employees must receive overtime pay when they work more than 40 hours in a workweek.

Human Rights Law: The name for some state and local anti-discrimination laws, such as the New York State Human Rights Law and New York City Human Rights Law.

I

I-9: A federal form that must be completed for each employee upon hire to ensure eligibility to work in the United States.

Impasse: The point in collective bargaining negotiations when the parties are unable to reach agreement and cannot make further compromise. Impasse may result in mediation, unilateral imposition, strike, lockout, or arbitration in different circumstances.

Implied contract: An obligation created by conduct rather than express agreement. For example, assurances of continued employment might create an implied employment contract in some situations.

Injunction: When a court orders a party to a dispute to take or refrain from taking particular action. In some employment cases, the court can even order the employer to reinstate an employee to the workforce.

Interactive process: When the employer and employee work together to determine whether a reasonable accommodation would permit the employee to perform the essential functions of the job. Per the ADA and other disability discrimination protections, employers must engage in an interactive process when they receive an accommodation request.

Intermittent leave: A form of leave (especially per the FMLA) where the employee takes time off on non-consecutive days, sometimes over an extended, even indefinite, period of time.

J

Joint employers: Separate entities that both employ the same employee(s).

Just cause: A valid reason for disciplining an employee. Usually required by collective bargaining agreements; sometimes required in individual employment contracts.

K

Key employee: Highly compensated personnel who may be subject to different rules, regulations, and entitlements than other employees. For example, employers may not have to offer a "key employee" reinstatement following FMLA leave. Also relevant to various tax issues.

L

Labor organization: An entity organized to engage with employers on behalf of employees about terms and conditions of employment. Includes, but is not technically limited to, labor unions.

Layoff: A reduction in the workforce based on economic or strategic business considerations. Labor attorneys usually distinguish between layoffs (temporary) and terminations (permanent).

Lockout: When an employer prevents employees from working, usually during a labor dispute. The company's counterpart to a strike by employees.

M

Management rights: Decisionmaking discretion reserved by the employer in its relationship with a labor organization. Usually applies to areas such as hiring, assigning, directing, and disciplining (with just cause) the workforce.

Mandatory subject of bargaining: Areas that employers and unions must bargain over if raised by the other side. Includes wages, hours, and other terms and conditions of employment.

Mass layoff: An event involving long-term loss of employment by many employees. Where enough employees are involved, advance notice may be required under federal and/or state Worker Adjustment and Retraining Notification (WARN) Acts.

Meal period: Time employees have off during their work shift to eat and rest. Usually governed by state law, a collective bargaining agreement, or employer policies.

Mediation: A dispute resolution procedure where a neutral mediator attempts to persuade the parties to resolve their disputes with a mutually acceptable outcome. Mediation can occur during collective bargaining, grievance resolution, and litigation.

Minimum wage: The lowest rate that employers may pay non-exempt employees. Can vary between federal and state, or even local laws. Employers must pay at least the highest applicable minimum wage to all employees.

Misconduct: Inappropriate behavior by an employee, usually in breach of a work rule or other stated or understood standard of conduct.

Misclassification: When an employer improperly treats an employee as an independent contractor or as exempt from overtime requirements. Either form of misclassification can result in significant liability to an employer.

Mitigation: Action by an employee that reduces the amount of damages recoverable from an employment discrimination claim. Employees usually have a duty to mitigate their damages, such as by seeking alternative employment.

N

National Labor Relations Act: A federal law giving non-government employees rights to engage in concerted activity, including joining a union. Enforced by the National Labor Relations Board (NLRB).

National origin discrimination: Discrimination prohibited by Title VII and some state anti-discrimination laws based on a person being from particular country or part of the world, having a certain ethnicity or accent, or appearing to be of a certain ethnic background.

NLRB: The National Labor Relations Board. A federal agency that oversees and enforces the National Labor Relations Act. Unlike most agencies, the NLRB dictates policy primarily by adjudication of cases rather than rulemaking.

Noncompetition agreement: A contract that restricts an employee from working for a competitor, usually during and within a certain period of time after the end of employment with a given employer. Often called a "non-compete."

Non-exempt: Term used to describe employees eligible to receive overtime under the FLSA or state laws. Can apply to both hourly and salaried employees, as well as those paid on another basis.

O

OFCCP: The Office of Federal Contract Compliance Programs. A division of the U.S. Department of Labor that enforces affirmative action requirements on entities that contract with the federal government.

Offer letter: Correspondence to a job applicant expressing willingness to hire the individual to work for the employer under certain terms. Sometimes the employee is asked to sign off on the offer letter. Other times an implied contract may arise based on the employee's acceptance of the position in reliance on the terms of the offer letter.

Organize: In the labor law context, to join a union for the purpose of collective bargaining with an employer.

OSHA: Either the Occupational Safety and Health Act or the Occupational Safety and Health Administration. Respectively, the federal law and agency that address workplace health and safety standards across the country.

Outside sales exemption: An exemption from minimum wage and overtime requirements for certain employees whose primary duty is making sales or obtaining orders or contracts for services or for the use of facilities. The employee must customarily perform this work outside of the employer's places of business.

Overtime: Extra time worked by employees for which they receive additional compensation. Under the FLSA, non-exempt employees must receive time-and-a-half their regular rate of pay for hours worked beyond 40 hours in a workweek. Collective bargaining agreements, company policy, employment contracts, or state laws may provide for overtime compensation in other circumstances.

P

Past practice: Unequivocal way of doing something regarding a workplace matter over a period of time. Sometimes arbitrators will enforce a past practice as a term and condition of employment under a collective bargaining agreement.

Permissive subject of bargaining: A topic that either side may raise in collective bargaining negotiations but may not insist on to impasse.

Pension: Money paid to retirees in recognition of their past service to an employer. Most commonly refers to a defined benefit arrangement, where the retiree receives a fixed amount of money based on time worked, salary history, etc. Defined contribution plans, like 401(k)'s, are increasingly more popular.

Picketing: An activity performed by employees involved in a labor dispute to demonstrate and seek public support for their position. Often involves employees carrying signs near the entrance to the employer's facility.

Plant closing: A shutdown of one or one or more facilities or operating units within an employment site. When a plant closing affects enough employees, the employer may have to provide advanced written notice under the federal or state WARN Act.

Prevailing wage: The hourly rate of pay that employers must pay to workers on covered public works projects. Usually varies based on location, job type, and other factors.

Probationary period: Time given to an employee at the beginning of employment to demonstrate ability to perform the job. Often used in nonunion workplaces, but more significant where a collective bargaining agreement makes it more difficult to remove an employee after the probationary period because the employee earns "just cause" protection.

Professional exemption: Employees performing jobs consistent with their advanced training in a particular field may be exempt from overtime under the FLSA and state law. Common examples of "professionals" include doctors, lawyers, teachers, accountants, and engineers.

Q

Qualified individual with a disability: A person who meets legitimate skill, experience, education, or other requirements of an employment position that he or she holds or seeks, and who can perform the essential functions of the position with or without reasonable accommodation. Such persons are eligible for protection from employment discrimination under the ADA.

Qualifying exigency: A circumstance in which an eligible employee may take FMLA leave based on a family member's current or upcoming active military duty. The FMLA does not contain an exhaustive list of qualifying exigencies, but they include issues arising from the military member's short-notice deployment, attending military events and related activities, and urgent childcare activities caused by the deployment.

Quantum meruit: From Latin for "as much as he deserved," a legal doctrine that may allow someone to recover a fair amount of compensation for work performed where the amount due has not been agreed on. A potential claim by an employee or independent contractor against an employer.

Quid pro quo: The form of sexual harassment involving a request for sexual activity in exchange for favorable job treatment.

R

Ratification: When the members of a bargaining unit approve a proposed collective bargaining agreement between their union and employer.

Reasonable accommodation: A change to the workplace or an employee's situation that will enable the employee to perform their job despite a disability. Employers must consider and make reasonable accommodations if they do not impose an undue hardship.

Regular rate: The rate from which time-and-a-half overtime compensation must be calculated under the FLSA. Derived from total remuneration, with some exclusions, divided by hours worked. Can include more than just the employee's base hourly rate, such as non-discretionary bonuses, shift premiums, etc.

Reinstatement: Rehiring of an employee. A potential remedy in employment discrimination cases, but more often ordered by an arbitrator who finds that the employer did not have just cause to terminate an employee under a collective bargaining agreement.

Religious accommodation: A change to the workplace or employee's situation based on an employee's religious beliefs and practices. Like with disability accommodation, employers must consider and make reasonable religious accommodations if they do not impose an undue hardship.

Replacement: A worker hired to work in place of an employee on strike. Replacements may either be permanent or temporary, subject to applicable labor laws.

Resignation: When an employee voluntarily ends employment with an employer. Usually distinguished from retirement because the employee intends to pursue another job.

Retaliation: Adverse action against an employee for engaging in protected activity, such a filing a discrimination complaint. Prohibited by most anti-discrimination laws and other employee protections.

Retirement: When an employee ends employment with an employer either at the end of their career or under other terms of an applicable retirement plan.

Right-to-work: State laws that prohibit unions from negotiating contract provisions requiring all employees to join the union. Just over half of the U.S. states are right-to-work states.

S

Seniority: A measure of an employee's length of service. In unionized workforces, seniority may determine compensation level, scheduling, and other aspects of employment.

Sexual harassment: Unwelcome treatment in the workplace based on one's sex. If it includes a request for sexual activity in exchange for favorable job treatment, then it is considered "quid pro quo" sexual harassment.

Severance: Money or other benefits paid to an employee upon termination of employment.

Strike: Refusal to work by a group of employees. Most often used by unions to gain leverage in negotiating terms and conditions of employment.

Subcontracting: Hiring an outside individual or group of workers to perform work rather than having the work done by an organization's own employees.

Successor: An entity that is legally responsible for one or more obligations of a previous entity with respect to employees. In some cases, a successor employer may be liable for discrimination by a former employer or may have to recognize a union that represented employees of a predecessor employer.

Supervisor: An employee with responsibility for other employees. An individual who qualifies as a supervisor under the National Labor Relations Act does not have the right to join a union. Supervisors might be exempt from overtime requirements, depending on other factors.

T

Termination: The end of employment. May be voluntary (e.g., retirement or resignation) or involuntary (e.g., firing).

Title VII: Part of the federal Civil Rights Act of 1964 that prohibits discrimination in employment on the basis of sex, race, color, religion, or national origin. Also prohibits retaliation for engaging in protected activity (e.g., filing a complaint) related to these categories.

U

Undue hardship: When an action requires significant difficulty or expense. If an otherwise reasonable accommodation would impose an undue hardship for an employer in a particular situation, then the employer may be excused from the obligation to make the accommodation.

Unemployment: Compensation available to some workers who have lost their jobs. Often provided through an insurance program run by state authorities.

Unfair labor practice: A violation of the National Labor Relations Act. Both employers and unions can be found to have committed an unfair labor practice.

Union: A labor organization representing workers with respect to terms and conditions of employment.

USERRA: The federal Uniformed Services Employment and Reemployment Rights Act of 1994. Generally, prohibits employment discrimination based on military status and requires employers to reinstate employees who have left work to perform military service.

V

Verbal warning: Form of discipline where an employee is formally told that their actions were inappropriate. Despite the name, verbal warnings are often also documented in the employee's personnel file.

Vesting: When an employee fully earns a benefit, usually related to retirement or stock ownership. Vesting typically depends on length of service, potentially among other factors.

Vicarious liability: Where the employer is held legally responsible for acts or omissions of its employees. For example, employers may be held liable for workplace harassment of an employee by co-workers if the employer knew or should have known of the harassment and failed to take appropriate action.

W

Wage: The amount of money that an employee earns for working a specific period of time. "Wage" is often used to refer to compensation of employees based on hours or days worked, whereas "salary" is more commonly used to describe fixed pay for a week or longer period.

Wage and hour laws: Collective term for laws that dictate minimum standards and requirements related to how much employees must be paid based on how much they work. Primarily includes state and federal minimum wage and overtime laws, including child labor laws, along with related recordkeeping requirements.

WARN Act: Either the federal Worker Adjustment and Retraining Notification Act or a similar state law. WARN Acts require covered employers to given advance written notice to employees, their union representatives (if applicable), and certain government officials before beginning employment actions that will result in loss of employment for groups of employees of at least certain numbers (as determined by the applicable law).

WARN notice: Term for the written notice given to employees, unions, and government officials in advance of plant closings or mass layoffs, or as otherwise required by a WARN Act.

Weingarten rights: Rights of unionized employees to request to have a union representative present for interviews that could result in discipline and of unions to assist employees in those interviews. *Weingarten* was a National Labor Relations Board case, and its holding only directly applies to private-sector employees covered by the National Labor Relations Act. The NLRB has gone back and forth on whether nonunion employees have similar rights to have a co-worker present. The principle also varies somewhat under state laws for employees not covered by the NLRA.

Whistleblower: An employee who reports their employer's alleged illegal actions to relevant authorities. Whistleblowers may receive protection under various state or federal laws.

Workers' compensation: Benefits (typically covering wage replacement and medical costs) available under state laws to employees who are injured through workplace accidents. Workers' compensation usually creates an exclusive remedy as against the employer in lieu of personal injury lawsuits by employees.

Written warning: Form of discipline where an employee is formally advised in writing that their actions were inappropriate. The employee is usually requested to sign the warning acknowledging their receipt and given the opportunity to add their comments to the document.

Wrongful termination: Claim by employee that the employer did not have a proper basis to end their employment. Could be based either on a statutory protection (e.g., discrimination) or a contractual just cause requirement.

Y

Years of service: Length of time that an employee has worked for the employer. Can be a determining factor for certain benefits, such as paid vacation time or severance pay.

Z

Zipper clause: A contractual provision in some collective bargaining agreement that precludes renegotiation of any terms of the agreement during its term.

INDEX

ABOUT THE AUTHOR

Scott P. Horton has been practicing labor and employment law since 2005. He graduated from the University of Virginia School of Law, where he was an editor on the Virginia Law Review. After more than a decade working in a large corporate law firm, he founded Horton Law PLLC in 2017. Scott lives with his wife and two children in Orchard Park, New York.

For more information, please visit HortonPLLC.com.

Made in the USA
Middletown, DE
05 March 2021